SPIRITUALITY *for a* RESTLESS CULTURE

SPIRITUALITY
for a RESTLESS
CULTURE

Ronald
Rolheiser

TWENTY-THIRD PUBLICATIONS
Mystic, Connecticut 06355

Twenty-Third Publications
185 Willow Street
P.O. Box 180
Mystic, CT 06355
(203) 536-2611
800-321-0411

ISBN 0-89622-469-4
Library of Congress Catalog Card No. 90-71753

Acknowledgments

Many persons have contributed to this book. I need to thank especially, however, my family who always support me, the Oblates of St. Mary's province who always trust me, Newman Theological College in Edmonton which has for years given me a job, an altar, a classroom, a desk, and a salary; thanks as well to the *Western Catholic Reporter* and the *Catholic Herald* which originally published many of these reflections. I also want to thank in a special way Delia Smith and Juliet Newport for generating interest among various London, England, publishers in these reflections. Finally, a big thanks to Neil and Pat Kluepfel and Helen Coleman at Twenty-Third Publications.

Preface

Thomas Merton, journaling during an extended period of solitude, wrote:

It is enough to be, in an ordinary human mode, with one's hunger and sleep, one's cold and warmth, rising and going to bed. Putting on blankets and taking them off, making coffee and then drinking it. Defrosting the refrigerator, reading, meditating, working, praying. I live as my ancestors have lived on this earth, until eventually I die. Amen. There is no need to make an assertion of my life, especially about it as mine, though doubtless it is not somebody else's. I must learn gradually to forget program and artifice. (Quoted in J.H. Griffin, *Follow the Ecstasy*, Latitudes Press, 1983).

Rarely is life enough for us. Rarely are we able to live restfully the spirit of our own lives. Most often what, where, and how we are living seems small, insignificant, petty, and depressingly domestic. We seldom notice our hunger and sleep, cold and warmth. Rarely do we taste the coffee we drink. Instead we go through our days too preoccupied, compulsive, driven, and dissatisfied to be present to and celebrate our own lives. Always, it seems, we are somehow missing out on life.

Add to this restlessness fear and guilt. We live always in fear—about losing life, losing health, losing loved ones, losing a job, losing securities, losing youth, losing respect, and losing ourselves. As well, our lives are always colored by guilt—guilt about things we have done and guilt about things we have not done. At times, too, we feel guilty simply for being alive, healthy, and experiencing life's pleasures.

For very few of us is human life a simple endeavor. Most of us understand only too clearly what St. Paul meant when he said, "For now we see as through a glass, darkly." We live as in an enigma, always partially away from home, longing to understand more fully and to be understood more fully. Slowly we tire of pilgrimage. We want to go home.

This book is a series of reflections that attempt, from many perspectives, to shed some light upon these problems. In essence they attempt to help a pilgrim home.

Margaret Atwood has said, "What touches you is what you touch." Accordingly these reflections touch on a whole lot of things, stuff of all kinds: restlessness, inconsummation, innocence and its loss, guilt and reconciliation, patience and chastity, death and loss, God's unconditional love, passion, friendship, love, sex, romance, community, social justice, human complexity and resiliency, weakness and depression, sin and conversion, the Eucharist, the martyrdom of obscurity, prayer, and the monasticism of daily life. These reflections attempt, however modestly, to formulate a spirituality for the restless.

Spirituality for a Restless Culture is for those who struggle to make this life, such as it is, enough. It is for those who ache to be outside themselves, with their headaches and heartaches behind them. It is dedicated to those who struggle with restlessness, guilt, and obsessions, who struggle to taste their own coffee and who struggle to feel the consolation of God.

Contents

Acknowledgments   *v*

Preface   *vii*

Chapter 1
Restlessness and Longing:
Culture vs. Spirituality   1

    Restless Hearts Yearn for God   2
    Longing Is Our Spiritual Lot   5
    The Martyrdom of Obscurity   8
    Staying Home on a Friday Night   11
    God Beats Small-time Blues   14
    Leaving God's Mark   17
    Curing Fire by Fire   20

Chapter 2
The Unfinished Symphony :
Dreams and Friendship   23

    The Unfinished Symphony   24
    Friendship Is Liberating Too   27
    Women, Men, and Friendship   30
    Emerging From Stone   33
    Dare to Be One in a Thousand   36
    Remembering as Surgery   39
    Single Life Offers Opportunities   42

Chapter 3
   Passion, Love, and Sex   45

       Romance Gives an Inkling of Heaven 46
       Passion Is God's Fire in Us 49
       Sexuality Is More Than Sex 52
       No Salvation in Sexology 55
       Three Phases of Fantasy 58

Chapter 4
   The Fire in One's Eyes:
   Losing and Recovering Innocence   61

       The Real Loss of Virginity 62
       Saying Yes to Santa Claus 65
       Don't Kill Santa Claus Too Soon 68
       Staring Chaos in the Face 71
       The Value of Fasting and Feasting 74

Chapter 5
   Prayer and the Monasticism of Daily Life   77

       The Monasticism of Daily Life 78
       Monasticism and the Playpen 81
       Just Too Busy to Bow Down 84
       Praying Through a Crisis 87
       Getting Angry With God 90

Chapter 6
  A Heart With Many Rooms:
  Social Justice   93

    The Bosom of God Is Not a Ghetto   94
    Closed to Love, Open to Hate   97
    Social Justice and Contemplation   100
    Make Your Welcome Hearty   103
    It's Easy to Sacrifice Others   107
    Alive with Prophetic Pain   110

Chapter 7
  Signs of the Times:
  Keeping One's Balance in a Complex World   113

    Keeping Your Faith in Balance   114
    Listening to Different Voices   117
    Being Normal Is Not Our Goal   120
    High Season for Religion Foes   123
    Abortion: No Quick Solutions   126
    Pro-life and Anti-abortion   129

Chapter 8
  Community and the Church:
  Commandments for the Long Haul   133

    Community—Our Greatest Need   134
    Can You Ever Really Leave Home?   137
    Some of Life's Questions   140
    Guidelines for the Long Haul   143

1

Restlessness and Longing: Culture vs. Spirituality

The only hope, or else despair
Lies in the choice of pyre or pyre—
To be redeemed from fire by fire.
Who then devised the torment? Love.
Love is the unfamiliar Name
Behind the hands that wove
The intolerable shirt of flame,
Which human power cannot remove.
We only live, only suspire
Consumed by either fire or fire.

T. S. Eliot, *Four Quartets*

Restless Hearts Yearn for God

We are fired into life by a madness that comes from our incompleteness. We awake to life tense, aching, erotic, full of sex and restlessness. This dis-ease is, singularly, the most important force within existence. It is the force for love and we are fundamentally shaped by our loves and deformed by their distortions. Shakespeare called this our "immortal longings" and poets, philosophers, and mystics have always recognized that, within it, there is precisely something of immortality.

Religiously, we have surrounded this longing with chastity and mystique. Ultimately our restless aching was seen as nothing less than the yearning within us for God. Augustine's interpretation of this eros was seen as the proper one: "You have made us for yourself, Lord, and our hearts are restless until they rest in you."

The longing was understood religiously: Adam, missing his rib, longing for Eve, man and woman, woman and man, longing for a primal wholeness in God and each other. This was high longing, eros as the spark of the divine in us, the fire from the anvil of God imprisoned inside us like a skylark, causing hopeless disquiet!

In the light of such diving restlessness we lived as pilgrims in time, longing for a consummation in a kingdom not fully of this world, caught, in Karl Rahner's words, "in the torment of the insufficiency of everything attainable, inconsummate, but knowing that here in this life all symphonies remain unfinished." In such a view, we pursued each other, embraced each other, and loved and made love to each other against the horizon of the infinite, under a high symbolic hedge. Love, romance, sex, and passion were sacred things, surrounded by much chastity and mystique.

Today that hedge is lower, the mystique and the chastity are less. We no longer embrace against the horizon of the infinite and our aches are no longer seen as longing for the transcendent.

Instead, for the most part, we have trivialized this longing, making it mean something much more concrete. The longing is for the good life, for good sex, for good successes, for what everybody else has, for the sweetening of life. There is little mystique in this. Plato, in his *Symposium*, tells of his students sitting around "telling wonderful stories of the meaning of their longing." Mystics, in their writings, tell of their deep longing for consummation within the body of Christ.

Today we rarely sit around and tell wonderful stories of the meaning of our longing, and ordinarily, there is little talk of aching for consummation within the body of Christ. Our stories are, for the most part, of yearnings more concretely channeled. It is a rare self-understanding today that lets one believe that his other aches and yearnings are mystical. We are not accustomed to think in such high terms; our symbols are more humble. Our aches and longings are seen as directed toward what we can attain, practically, in the here and now: achievement, success, sex, limited love and enjoyment.

There is nothing bad about these things, but in the end, if we define our deepest longings as directed toward them in themselves, we end up in despair. Eventually, we no longer believe that we can recover a primal wholeness through the embrace of another, the perpetuity of our seed, and the contemplation of God. We lower our sights. We trivialize our longing.

We no longer see our longing as a congenital and holy restlessness put in us by God to push us toward the infinite. Instead it becomes a tamed and tame thing, domesticated, an-

aesthetized, and distracted. We are restless only in a tired way
(which drains us of energy) and not in a divine way (which
gives us energy).

And so we should ask ourselves, What kind of lovers are
we?

Are we still fired into life by a madness that lets us understand the insatiability of our hearts as a call to infinite love? Do
we still see ourselves as pursuing each other, embracing each
other, and loving each other against the horizon of the infinite?
Do we still understand ourselves as meeting on holy ground
with all the mystique and chastity that this implies?

Or do we believe that life is best lived without such mysticism, high romance, high eros, and high chastity? Do we still
tell each other wonderful stories of the meaning of our longings, or do we discourage each other from raising our eyes
above the immediate?

Do we cry with each other and support each other in the
frustration of our incompleteness, or do we give each other the
impression that there is something wrong with us because our
lives are inconsummate and our symphonies are incomplete?
Do we still take our longings and emptiness to God in prayer,
or do we demand that life gives us, here and now, the full
symphony?

Do we lovingly and gratefully receive the spirit of our own
lives, despite the tensions, or do we live in angry jealousy? Are
we loving against an infinite horizon, or is our eros directed
only toward the concrete sweetening of life?

What kind of lovers are we?

Longing Is Our Spiritual Lot

On February 12, 1944, thirteen-year-old Anne Frank wrote the following words in her now famous diary:

> Today the sun is shining, the sky is a deep blue, there is a lovely breeze and I am longing—so longing —for everything. To talk, for freedom, for friends, to be alone And I do so long...to cry! I feel as if I am going to burst, and I know that it would get better with crying; but I can't, I'm restless, I go from room to room, breathe through the crack of a closed window, feel my heart beating, as if it is saying, "Can't you satisfy my longing at last?"
>
> I believe that it is spring within me, I feel that spring is awakening, I feel it in my whole body and soul. It is an effort to behave normally, I feel utterly confused. I don't know what to read, what to write, what to do, I only know that I am longing.

There is in all of us, at the very center of our lives, a tension, an aching, a burning in the heart that is insatiable, non-quietable, and very deep. Sometimes we experience this longing as focused on a person, particularly if we are in a love that is not consummated. Other times we experience this yearning as a longing to attain something.

Most often, though, it is a longing without a clear name or focus, an aching that cannot be clearly pinpointed or described. Like Anne Frank, we only know that we are restless, full of disquiet, aching at a level we cannot seem to get at.

When we look into history, philosophy, poetry, mysticism, and literature we see an astonishing variety of ways in which this aching is expressed.

For instance, many of us have read Richard Bach's little parable *Jonathan Livingston Seagull*. This book spoke deeply to millions of people. It is a very simple story: Jonathan is a seagull who, when he comes to consciousness, is not satisfied with being a seagull. He looks at his life and the lives of other seagulls, and he finds it too small: "All a seagull ever does is eat and fight!" So Jonathan tries to burst out. He tries to fly higher, to fly faster, to do anything that might break the asphyxiating limits of being a seagull. He does not know what he wants; he only knows that he is hopelessly restless, that he must break out. Many times he crashes and almost kills himself, but he keeps trying.

This is a story obviously more of the human heart than of a seagull. It describes our search, our aching, our congenital propensity for the limitless, the free, the total embrace.

In more abstract ways, this has been expressed in history: Philosophers speak of "a desire of the part to return to the whole"; mystics speak of "the spark of the divine in us"; the ancient Greeks spoke of something they called *nostos*, homesickness (a feeling of never being at home, even when you are at home).

The Vikings called it "wanderlust," the insatiable need to push further and further into the horizon; Shakespeare talked of "immortal longings"; Gerard Manley Hopkins called the human spirit "an imprisoned skylark"; Augustine prayed to God: "You have made us for yourself, Lord, and our hearts are restless until they rest in you"; e.e. cummings said, "For every mile the feet go, the heart goes nine."

All of these feelings are in all of us. We are all deeply and hopelessly subject to dis-ease, incapable in this life of finding lasting rest. This restlessness, however, must never be seen as something that sets us against what is spiritual, religious, and of God.

In fact this hopeless aching and lack of ease is the very basis of the spiritual life. What we do with the eros inside us, be it heroic or perverse, is our spiritual life.

The tragedy is that so many persons, full of riches and bursting with life, see this drive as something essentially irreligious, as something that sets them against what is spiritual. Nothing could be further from the truth. Our erotic impulses are God's lure in us. They are our spirit!

We experience them precisely as "spirit," as soul, as that which makes us more than mere animals. Our soul is not an invisible kind of tissue floating around within us, that stains when we sin and cleanses when we are in grace and that ultimately floats away from the body after death. Our soul is our eros, our minds and hearts in their deep restlessness.

Living the tension that arises out of that is the spiritual life. In that sense, everyone has a spiritual life—either a good one or a destructive one. Our spirits make it impossible for us to be static; we must move outside ourselves.

That movement outwards (which is experienced as a double tension: a hunger that drives us outwards and an attractive outside person or object that draws us outwards) is either beneficial to us or destructive. When it is beneficial, we have a good spiritual life; when it is destructive, we have a bad one.

It is important, therefore, that we do not identify the spiritual life with something exotic (for religious fanatics), extraordinary (for professional contemplatives), or as something not for those who are full-blooded and full of eros.

It is non-negotiable. If you are alive, you are restless, full of spirit. What you do with that spirit is your spiritual life.

The Martyrdom of Obscurity

We crave few things as deeply as self-expression.

Deep within the eros that makes us restless and dissatisfied lies the incurable need to express ourselves, to be known, recognized, understood, and seen by others as unique and as having deep riches inside us.

Self-expression, being known and experienced in our depth, is vital to living and loving. A heart that is unknown, unappreciated in its depth, and lacking in meaningful self-expression is always a restless and frustrated heart. It is normally, too, a competitive and bitter one. But meaningful self-expression is difficult and full self-expression is impossible.

In the end all of us live in obscurity, unknown, frustrated. Our lives are always smaller than our needs and our dreams. Ultimately we all live in small towns, no matter where we live; and save for a few brief moments of satisfaction, spend most of our lives waiting for a fuller moment to come, waiting for a time when we will be less hidden.

From this frustration stems a tremendous restlessness and dissatisfaction. Each of us would like to be the famous writer, the graceful ballerina, the admired athlete, the movie star, the cover girl, the renowned scholar, the Nobel prize winner, the household name. But in the end each of us is just another unknown, living with other unknowns, collecting an occasional autograph.

Our lives always seem too small for us. We sense ourselves as extraordinary persons living very ordinary lives. Because of this sense of obscurity we are seldom satisfied, easeful, and happy with our lives. There is always, too, much still inside us that wants expression, that needs recognition, that feels that something very precious, unique, and rich is living and dying in futility.

And in truth, seen only from the perspective of this world, much that is precious, unique, and rich is living and dying in futility. Only a rare few achieve meaningful self-expression. There is a certain martyrdom in this. Iris Murdoch has said, "Art has its martyrs, not the least of which are those who have preserved their silence." Lack of self-expression, whether chosen or imposed by circumstances, is a real death. Like all death, however, it can be paschal or terminal. If merely accepted as inevitable it leads to bitterness and a broken spirit. If linked to the paschal mystery of Christ, if it is seen as an opportunity to enter the hidden life of Christ, it leads to a new ease in life, to restfulness; and it lays the axe to the root of our competitiveness, anger, and bitterness. Today we are called as Christians to the martyrdom of obscurity. Christianity always invites its adherents to martyrdom. To be a follower of Christ demands that one lay down one's life. But this takes various forms.

For Jesus and his apostles, as for many early Christians during the times of the persecutions, martyrdom meant physical death. They had to give up the possibilities that this life offered in order to remain true to a more distant possibility — permanent intimacy with God and each other. In dying they entered the hidden life of Christ. That type of martyrdom is still being asked of Christians in many parts of the world, notably in Latin America.

In North America and Western Europe, however, at least of many of us, a different kind of martyrdom is being asked. Our culture persecutes its Christians in a different way. Affluence and leisure have created a higher psychic temperature. These have focused us on interpersonal, sexual, artistic, athletic, and scientific achievement. In a word, they have focused us on self-expression. In our culture meaningful self-expression is everything; lack of it is death. Yet it is this death that paschally we must enter.

Not that we should, in the name of the Gospel, be uncreative, unresourceful, phlegmatic, or stoic under-achievers. But we should, in the name of the Gospel, enter the hidden life of Christ. Within it the current of eros that drives us mercilessly toward self-expression can be more properly channeled, so that we do not go through life unhealthily competitive, bitter, angry, hopelessly restless, not at ease, and basically unhappy because we are ordinary and obscure. Only when we enter the martyrdom of obscurity will our ordinary lives be enough.

Thomas Merton, after several years in a hermitage, wrote: "It is enough to be, in an ordinary human mode....I must learn to live so as gradually to forget programme and artifice."

Ordinary life can be enough for us, but only if we first undergo the martyrdom of obscurity and enter Christ's hidden life. It is not easy, however. In many ways it is easier to sacrifice life itself than to sacrifice dreams.

Staying Home on a Friday Night

I am old enough to have known another time. Things were different when I was little. Many of life's pleasures were not available and people made do, celebrating what there was to celebrate and not over-expecting. Back then few expected or demanded the whole pie. Heaven was seen as something for later.

My parents and their generation lived a simple spiritual philosophy: This life is but a short time of waiting, "mourning and weeping in a vale of tears!" It is not so important to be happy.

Today there are sneers about their tears. But that somber philosophy of theirs got them through life with their faith and loves intact and, ironically, probably equipped them with a greater capacity for enjoyment and happiness than we possess today.

There is today too little talk, in our churches and in our world, about the "vale of tears" and the incompleteness of our present lives. Spiritualities of the resurrection and psychologies of self-actualization, whatever their other strengths, no longer give us permission to be in pain, to be unwhole, ill, unattractive, aged, unfulfilled, or even just alone on a Friday night.

The idea is all too present that we can only be happy if we somehow fulfill every hunger within us, if our lives are completely whole, consummated, and we are never alone on a Friday night. Unless every pleasure that we yearn for can be tasted we cannot be happy.

Because of this we over-expect. We stand before life and love in a greedy posture and with unrealistic expectations, demanding the resolution of all our eros and tension. However, life in this world can never give us that.

We are pilgrims on earth, exiles journeying toward home. The world is passing away. We have God's word for it. And we need God's word for it! Too much in our experience today militates against the fact that here in this life all symphonies remain unfinished.

Somehow we have come to believe that a final solution for the burning tensions within us lies within our present grasp. I am not sure who or what gives us this idea. Maybe it is the movie and television industries with their leading men and leading ladies who are presented to us as already redeemed, persons who are gorgeous, immersed in life and meaning, and who have the wherewithal within their grasp to taste whatever life has to offer.

But something has led us to the belief that we need not put up with tension and frustration and that there are persons in this life who are already enjoying a redeemed life.

That belief, however unconscious and unexpressed, lies at the root of much of our restlessness and unhappiness today. None of us is whole, not even our gorgeous leading men and ladies. Yet because we believe that somehow we can or should be whole, we go through life denigrating what chances we have for rest and happiness.

A simple example serves to illustrate: In our culture we suffer from what might be termed "Friday night syndrome." Few people can stay home quietly and rest on a Friday night. Why? Is it because we are not tired and ideally could not appreciate a nice quiet time? No! We cannot stay home quietly on a Friday night because inside us moves a restless demon that assures us that everyone in the whole world is doing something exciting on Friday night. Once that voice is heard, then our homes, our families, and our commitments begin to look unexciting. Peace and restfulness slip away and we are caught up in an insatiable restlessness.

This example illustrates the basic principle: So much of our unhappiness comes from comparing our lives, our friendships, our loves, our commitments, our duties, our bodies, and our sexuality to some idealized and non-Christian vision of things that falsely assures us that there is a heaven on earth. When that happens, and it does, our tensions begin to drive us mad, in this case to a cancerous restlessness.

In a culture (and, at times, in a church) that tells us that no happiness is possible unless every ache and restlessness inside us is fulfilled, how hard it is to be happy.

How tragic it is to be alone! How tragic it is to be unmarried! How tragic it is to be married, but not completely fulfilled romantically and sexually! How tragic it is not to be good-looking! How tragic it is to be unhealthy, aged, handicapped! How tragic it is to be caught up in duties and commitments, small children and diapers and routine, which limit our freedom and relationships! How tragic it is to be poor! How tragic it is to go through life and not be able to taste every pleasure on earth! It almost isn't worth living!

There is wisdom and, yes, even comfort, in the old "mourning and weeping in this vale of tears" philosophy. Sometimes that expression was abused and people forgot that the Creator did not just make us for life after death. He did also intend some life after birth! But those who lived that philosophy generally did not attempt to milk life for more than it could give them. Those who lived that philosophy were a lot less restless and greedy for experience than we are today. They could much more restfully enjoy God's great gifts—life, love, youth, health, friendship, and sexuality—even as they are limitedly given in this life. Those who lived that philosophy were, I am sure, much more restful on Friday nights!

God Beats Small-time Blues

Sigmund Freud stated that neurosis is the disease of the normal person and that everyone is neurotic to some degree. This
is true if one defines neurosis as he did, simply as meaning
that one suffers more than one needs to. Neurosis, for him, is
more a dis-ease than a disease.

For Freud, this dis-ease comes about because of the repression of sex. In his understanding we are so hopelessly and incurably sexed, with such limited access for sexual expression,
that we are forced to repress most of our erotic energies. Eventually these repressed energies dominate and preoccupy our
lives in a negative way. Everyone, subsequently, lives in a fundamental dis-ease.

There is certainly some truth in that.

More recently thinkers such as Martin Heidegger and Ernest
Becker have argued that we are all neurotic, but have suggested that the root of our dis-ease is not so much repressed sexuality as the repression of our fear of death. For them, we have a
deep sense of our own mortality and, consciously and unconsciously, repress it. Eventually this causes a neurosis that robs
us of the full joy of living because we are afraid of dying.
Again, obviously, there is much truth in this.

More recently still, a number of psychologists and novelists,
among others, have suggested that there is a different reason
why we are fundamentally dis-eased. For them, while repressed sexuality and fear of death certainly unsettle our lives
and cause untold restlessness, they are not the real reason why
our lives are seldom peaceful and contented. They submit that
our neurotic restlessness has another cause. In our Western
world we live in a culture that stresses the importance and significance of the individual, while at the same time downplay-

ing the importance of God. These two emphases, the significance of the individual life and the absence of God, cannot go together without creating an intolerable restlessness inside each of us. A fundamental dis-ease results when the truths that are revealed by God are taught in a world that postures independence of God.

What happens when we are raised to believe that we are, each of us, precious, special, and meant to leave a lasting mark on this earth...and we live in a world in which we are obscure, unknown, homogenized, taken for granted, and deprived of meaningful self-expression? What happens when we are taught that our lives have deep significance and that our personalities, our dreams, our pains, our joys, and our loves have infinite importance...and we live in a world that cannot give us this sense?

What happens inside us when we sense how precious are our individual stories, in all their unique intricacies, and we live in a world that is not interested in our stories and is bored when we begin to speak of ourselves?

What happens when we are told by our world that our daydreams are true and that we are infinitely precious, but that same world, precisely because it no longer relies on God to give us that preciousness, cannot offer us a sense of specialness?

What happens? In brief, we get very restless. We become deeply and hopelessly dissatisfied. The joys that our lives do give us tend to pale and be insignificant because we feel that they, and we, are small-time, small-town, obscure, too little known and recognized.

We end up frustrated, feeling trapped in a domesticity that excludes us from where we would like to be and from whom we would like to be with. Our families and friends do not satisfy us because they, like ourselves, seem small-time. They are too much like us to be of help in our restlessness. We crave relationships with the famous, the powerful, the achievers, with those who have attained significance in the world's eyes and whose stories the world deems precious and interesting.

We become obsessed with the need for self-expression, with the need for achieving something unique and lasting. We fear dying without leaving a permanent mark.

Our daily lives seem poor and uninteresting, and we live so much of our lives waiting, waiting for someone or something or some moment to come along and give us significance and preciousness. Our world teaches us that we are significant and precious, but then deprives us of the one thing that can make us so, God. This sets off an incurable ache.

A sense of our individual significance and a lack of a sense of God cannot go together without creating a restless and intolerable dis-ease. Only God can give us the sense of our own preciousness and ultimate significance. Only in a life rooted deeply in prayer, where we can live contentedly hidden in Christ and, there, accept the martyrdom of obscurity, will our aching and dissatisfaction cease and our dis-ease give way to restful contentment.

Leaving God's Mark

We nurse within our hearts the hope that we are different, that we are special, that we are extraordinary. We long for the assurance that our birth was no accident, that a god had a hand in our coming to be, that we exist by divine fiat. We ache for a cure for the ultimate disease of mortality. Our madness comes when the pressure is too great and we fabricate a vital lie to cover up the fact that we are mediocre, accidental, mortal. We fail to see the glory of the Good News. The vital lie is unnecessary because, as Alan Jones reminds us in *Journey into Christ*, all things we truly long for have been freely given us.

All of us, I am sure, know what is meant by those words. On the one hand we sense that we are extraordinary, creatures under divine providence, precious and significant, irrespective of our practical fortunes in life. We sense that we are not mere evolutionary accidents, simple victims of fate, chance, luck, randomness, and accident, doomed to disappear forever. Deep down there is the feeling that we are God's children, under God's providence, loved and called to a birth, life, meaning, and significance that is unique and infinitely precious. We sense too that we are precious not on the basis of what we accomplish or achieve during our lives, but simply on the basis of being created and loved by God.

But this intuition, however deeply felt, normally wilts under the pressure of trying to live a life that is unique and special in a world in which billions of others are also trying to do the same thing. Can billions be infinitely precious and utterly unique?

In the end mediocrity, anonymity, and mortality overwhelm us. We begin to fear that we are not precious nor under divine providence. There is instead the sense that we are merely mediocre hacks trying to make the world believe that we are something different. One among billions of others, clawing and scratching for a little uniqueness, meaning, and immortality!

When we feel like this, we begin to believe that we are precious and unique only when we accomplish something that precisely sets us apart and ensures that we are remembered. For most of us the task of adult life is that of guaranteeing our own preciousness, lovableness, meaning, immortality, and sanctity. In the end we do not believe that we have these, independent of our own accomplishments. Hence we cannot, without bitter frustration, live ordinary lives of anonymity, hidden in Christ.

Few things torment us and are as destructive of our peace and happiness as is this problem: We have set ourselves the impossible, frustrating task of assuring for ourselves something that only God can give us. Because of this, ordinary life does not seem enough for us, and we live as restless, competitive, driven persons who are forced, precisely, to fabricate a lie to cover up the fact that we are mediocre.

Why is ordinary life not enough for us? Why does it always seem that our lives are small-town, small-time, too insignificant, not exciting enough? Why do we habitually feel mediocre, dissatisfied, unhappy at being like everyone else? Why the propensity to leave our mark? Why is there such a torment in the insufficiency of everything attainable? Why does our own situation so often feel oppressively domestic?

Why, like Jonathan Livingston Seagull, do we want to fly above the rest, to leave the pack behind, and to somehow be more special than others? Why can we not embrace each other as sisters and brothers and, in humility and gratitude, rejoice in each other's gifts and each other's existence? Why the feeling that the other is a rival? Why the need for masks, for pretence, for hype, for all kinds of lies that let us project certain images about ourselves?

Because we are trying to give ourselves something that only God can give us: ultimate uniqueness, significance, and immortality.

Protestantism has always proclaimed that the central part of Christ's message is the statement: "Faith alone saves." We are justified by faith alone. They are right. That simple line reveals the secret, namely, that God gives eternal life. Preciousness, meaning, significance, and immortality are free gifts from God.

If we could believe that we would become a whole lot more restful, peaceful, humble, less competitive, grateful, and happy, we would no longer hopelessly pursue the search for the holy grail. Ordinary life, in all its domesticity, shared with billions of others, would contain enough to ensure our preciousness, meaning, and significance.

Ordinary life is enough. Preciousness and significance come from being lived by God, not from what we can achieve. In the end we are not mediocre, and there is no need to fabricate the vital lie.

Curing Fire by Fire

In his *Four Quartets*, T. S. Eliot contrasts two kinds of fire:
    The only hope, or else despair
    Lies in the choice of pyre or pyre—
    To be redeemed from fire by fire.

What Eliot captures here is the deepest and most painful of all human choices, the alternative between God's flames and those of our own making. What is implied here?

We are born dis-eased, erotic, full of tension, relentlessly restless, full of fire. To be a human being is to be on fire for a consummation, a restfulness, a love, a symphony that, in this life, perpetually escapes us. In every cell of our bodies and in every area of our minds and hearts there is a fire, a restless ache, a burning for someone or something we have not yet experienced.

What comes naturally to us because of this is restless and compulsive activity. Being on fire, we are greedy for experience and find it hard ever to be satisfied or to come to rest. So much of what we do in life comes not from a free center inside us but from restlessness and compulsiveness. We are perpetually dissatisfied and unable to live within the spirit of our own lives. Our lives seem always to be too small, too petty, too domestic, too unimportant because we are on fire for bigger things, more important jobs, more important places.

Moreover, this fire, this relentless restlessness, does not necessarily suggest that somehow we are living wrongly. Its source is our own depth, the infinite caverns of our minds and hearts. Philosophers and anthropologists have always distinguished human from beast on the basis of rationality. In my own anthropology classes I like to phrase that somewhat more humorously by stating that the difference between human and beast is that animals munch grass contentedly in meadows while humans smoke it discontentedly in bars...therein lies the difference! And that difference issues from different depths of mind and heart. Animals are not deep, humans are.

Given our infinite depth and our infinite hungers, in this life we will always be on fire. The fire inside us will never be extinguished by attaining the right experiences—the right partner in love, the right job, the right city, the right friends, the right recognition. Our choice is not between restlessness and restfulness, but between two kinds of restlessness, between two kinds of fire: "pyre and pyre."

We are destined to be consumed by one kind of fire or another, but the flames are very different—God's flames or those of our own choosing.

The solution to our restlessness, our fire, is to let it be consumed and transformed by a higher fire, a higher eros, a higher restlessness, the eros of God.

What is implied here? In a nutshell, what is meant is that we must widen our longings, deepen our aches, raise further still our psychic temperature so that we burn precisely for the final consummation, the final symphony, God's kingdom.

Several years ago, after giving a conference on celibacy to a group of seminarians, I was approached by one of them with this complaint: "I am tired of abstract talk about sexuality. It's all useless because nobody can tell us what to actually do with sexual tension."

What can be done with unresolved tension, sexual or otherwise? We can pick it up, enter it, widen and deepen it, and let it be transformed by something still deeper: Christ's loneliness. Fire must be redeemed by fire, eros by eros, aching by aching, frustration by advent, restless compulsion by gestation.

Great spiritual writers have always told us that we should imitate Christ not by trying to look as he looked, or even by trying to do the precise things that he did. Rather we should imitate Christ by trying to feel as he felt, by trying to imitate his motivation, that is, his deep longing for the consummation of everybody and everything in one community of love and peace.

That feeling is a fire, a restlessness, an ache, an eroticism. But it is a fire that does not lead to a compulsive greed for experience or to a restless incapacity to receive the spirit of one's own life. Rather it is a restlessness that leads one to genuinely live in advent, that is, to become pregnant with the gifts of the Holy Spirit—charity, joy, peace, patience, goodness, long-suffering, constancy, mildness, and chastity—and gestate the conditions within which all fire and longing can be consumed by the fire and longing of God.

Who then devised the torment? Love.

2

The Unfinished Symphony:
Dreams and Friendship

What you dream alone remains a dream,
what you dream with others can become reality.

Edward Schillebeeckx

The Unfinished Symphony

Strange what meaning lies in paradox and anomaly! In defeat there is a victory, in humiliation there is glory, in confusion there is always a new clarity, in the absurd one finds meaning, in tears lie relief, and in virtually every death there is new and deeper life.

Recently I wrote an article about a young woman making her perpetual commitment as a religious sister. I stated both how much I admired her for the courage and vision to make such vows within a culture that rejects them and how much these vows themselves have a clarity and beauty precisely because they make the truth they express repellent and so drive all who witness them inwards, forcing them to assimilate the truth in a new way. I have been the recipient of some strange looks and questions since. Repellent vows? Really!

I am not without gratitude for this critique because it has forced me to clarify something I had just dimly felt but could not express, until now. Now, with some help from an answer Thomas Merton once gave to an interviewer who asked him how he felt about celibacy, I want to spell out what is inchoately expressed in that term "repellent."

I will focus on just one of the vows, celibacy, because it is generally within that vow that one experiences this repellency in all its poignancy —and it is within that vow that the greatest danger for pathology lies. The principle involved in living that vow applies as well to poverty and obedience.

A celibate life is of itself an absurdity, pure and simple. Man without woman and woman without man is absurd.

"It is not good for the man to be alone!" When God spoke those words he meant them for everyone for ever. To be celibate is to live in incompleteness, unwholeness, and inconsummation, in a loneliness that God himself has damned.

Further, this is not merely a matter of celibates having or not having good interpersonal relations. A vision prevalent today contends that good heterosexual or homosexual friendships and a supportive community can and should offset the pain and unnaturalness of celibacy. After all, sexuality is more than just having sex and celibates need not be excluded from the realm of loving.

There is some truth in that, some wisdom, but also a lot of naivety. Friendship and supportive community are critical, in the long run more important than sex. But that fact does not offset the emotional crucifixion of celibacy because it cannot bypass the fact that however good and supportive community may be, within these, the members do not make a one, nor come to a consummation, in a way that satisfies the condition of Genesis: "That is why a man leaves his father and his mother and clings to his wife and the two become one flesh."

In a sexual relationship within a marriage a man and a woman make one in a way that a man and a woman (or a woman and a woman or a man and a man) do not make one in any unmarried friendship or community, however deep these latter relationships may be.

Hence outside married sexual relationship one will always live in a loneliness that has been condemned by the Creator.

However, I suspect, and I know from my married friends, that this loneliness exists too within marriage, even within the best of marriages. Within a good marriage there are moments when loneliness is transcended, but these moments are brief and usually point to a further, more difficult, place where, ultimately, two lonely and unconsummated, though married, persons elect to save one another from absurdity by being absurd together—for life. Hence what I write here applies as well to married persons.

At this point I suspect the tone of this section must sound masochistic. But this is not a masochistic answer. It is in freely accepting this limit, this pathos, that we rise above ourselves and become more human, because it is then that we let go of those imaginings and unrealistic expectations that prevent us from living in advent for God's kingdom.

But this implies that we stop lying. The celibate condition, in the course of time, has become encrusted with pious lies, just as the married one has become encrusted with a false romanticism. The lies and the romanticism serve to hide the real pain, the real tragedy, and the real meaning and nobility of both vocations because they hide the fact that in both celibacy and marriage the symphony remains unfinished. A damned loneliness always exists. We remain painfully sexed, separate, partially always alone.

Only when this foolishness is recognized does inconsummation become thirst for a wider life; then self-pity turns into hope, confusion into clarity, foolishness into beauty. Then absurdity becomes a center of peace and there, finally, things begin to make some sense and both marriage and celibacy become possible and beautiful.

Friendship Is Liberating Too

I was raised to believe that prayer and private morality were the foundations of the spiritual life. They were non-negotiable. You were considered a good Christian if you prayed, privately and liturgically, and if your private morals were in order.

The Catholicism I was raised on, while never denying the importance of social justice, rarely impressed upon me the fact that involvement with the struggle of the poor was just as non-negotiable as prayer and private morality.

The conscience of Christianity has changed. Perhaps the most critical development within all Christianity these past years has not been the changes brought in by Vatican II but the re-emergence of the idea that there can be no spiritual health without social justice.

Liberation theologians from the Third World and social justice advocates within our own culture have helped irrevocably re-impress into the Christian conscience the idea that social justice is non-negotiable, that it is not an extra we can choose to get involved in or not, just as prayer and private morality are not optional. To be a healthy Christian means to pray, to live a good moral life, and to be involved with the poor. All three of these are non-negotiable. But this is not so easily conceded by all, as recent tensions within the church show.

Social justice movements are often accused of not emphasizing sufficiently private conversion, private prayer, and private morality. The criticism is made that they are producing a spirituality with an underdeveloped private conscience—that is, it does not matter whether you pray, hold grudges, are one-sided, live sexually beyond the commandment, or attend church or not, as long as you work for the right causes.

Conversely, on their part, they make the criticism that, for the most part, Christianity has dangerously privatized conversion and produced a spirituality with an underdeveloped social conscience—namely, you are a good Christian as long as you say your prayers and attend church and obey the church's sexual commandments, irrespective of whether you are ignoring or even positively exploiting the poor.

There is some truth and some exaggeration in the accusations of both sides, though at this time, because of an imbalance in the direction of private conversion, I submit, the church must be more sensitive to criticism made by the proponents of social justice. Their criticism, save for a few exaggerated expressions, is correct and biting.

Why is it that a Christian may not, in good conscience, ignore the teachings of Scripture and the church regarding prayer and private morality, and yet she or he may, in good conscience, ignore the social teachings of Scripture and the church?

Thus, for example, the church's teachings that have to do with sexual ethics (e.g., *Humanae Vitae*) tend to be seen as the deciding criteria determining who is good or bad as a Christian, while the church's teaching on social issues (e.g., *Mater et Magistra*) that have equal moral and dogmatic authority can be largely ignored in good conscience.

That's an imbalance in need of correction. But here is still a further imbalance:

Through much pain, we have come to realize that prayer alone is not enough; social justice is also needed. Now, through more pain, we are coming to realize that prayer and social justice, together but alone, are also not enough.

Why do I say this? Because too many persons who both pray and do social justice are angry, bitter, lacking in gratitude and joy, and full of hate. What is lacking? In a word, friendship. A healthy spiritual life is anchored on three pillars, prayer, social justice, and friendship. The latter is as critical and non-negotiable as the former two. Without the warming and mellowing that good friendship brings into life, we invariably lose gratitude and joy.

To pray and to do social justice is to be prophetic. But that's a lonely and hard business. Prophets are persecuted, are powerless, and are rejected. Because of this, it is all too easy to get angry, to feel self-righteous, to fill with bitterness, to become selective in our prophecy, and to hate the very people we are trying to save.

When this happens, gratitude and joy disappear from our lives and we are unable to live without the need to be angry. Invariably, then, both our prayer and social action become perverse. We become recognized not for our joy and love, but for our anger and bitterness. Our prophetic words are spoken not out of love and grief, but out of indignation. We turn poverty into an ideology by losing sight of the end of the struggle—namely, celebration, joy, play, embrace, forgiveness.

Only friendship can save us. Loving, challenging friends who can melt our bitterness and free us from the need to be angry are as critical within the spiritual life as are prayer and social justice. To neglect friendship is to court bitterness and perversion.

There are three key questions to ask ourselves when we are evaluating spiritual health:

1. Do I pray every day?
2. Am I involved with the struggle of the poor?
3. Do I have the kinds of friendships in my life that move me beyond bitterness and anger?

Women, Men, and Friendship

The German poet Rainer Maria Rilke once wrote: "Perhaps the sexes are more similar than we think...and thus the great renewal of our world consists in this: that man and maid, freed from all false feeling and aversion, might come together as friends, as neighbors, as more than lovers—as brothers and sisters." One of the deep wounds in Western culture is that men and women find it very hard to be friends. It's easy for them to be lovers, but not friends.

I don't know how often I have had people of both sexes complain to me about the difficulty of finding friendship with the opposite sex. Invariably the comment is: "It is so much easier to find a lover than a friend." That is normally, too, spoken with a touch of sadness. Good, healthy, open, chaste, life-giving heterosexual friendship is rare. It is not that we do not crave it or value it, it is just that we rarely find it. Why?

At one level the answer is easy. Sexual tension takes away easefulness. Consciously and unconsciously, every deep heterosexual friendship is partly manipulated by sexual tension. We need not be unduly apologetic about this.

In heterosexual friendships there will be tensions, hesitations, awkwardness, inhibitions, and hidden agendas. Sex is too powerful to allow men and women to be easily honest and up front in friendship. Everything is sexually charged and so nearly every action can be taken to imply something else and, consequently, there is a lot of cautiousness in our reaching out to each other.

That caution is often well-founded. We should not be naive about the power of sexuality. There is a natural dynamism within sexuality that pushes toward genitality. Deep relationships between men and women, by nature, cry out for sexual consummation. That is deep within instinct and written into the very way God made us. This makes our coming together as friends very difficult.

But there are other reasons for this difficulty beyond the natural incurable push of sexuality itself. To the natural dis-ease of sexuality, our culture adds a pansexuality and an obsession with genitality. Today virtually everything has a sexual innuendo, and having sex is, more or less, an extension of dating. In such a setting, our understanding of life, sex, and friendship narrows. The Greeks saw six aspects to love: *eros*, sexual attraction, falling in love; *ludus*, playfulness, love as a game; *philia*, friendship, care; *mania*, obsessional love, infatuation, dark eros; *pragma*, sensible, committed love; and *agape*, selfless, altruistic love.

Our culture tends to define love basically in terms of eros and mania. To love someone is to be romantically obsessed with them and to want sex with them. When this is true, then sexuality quickly becomes just sex. It is no longer understood, first and foremost, as a dimension of self-awareness, as a hunger of the soul for wholeness, community, family, creativity, friendship, affection, and play.

In our culture's view, a view we have generally interiorized and made our own, to love means to make love, to be a lover. Platonic heterosexual friendships are seen as too incomplete, too empty, or as simply unrealistic. No wonder men and women find it hard to be in deep friendship with each other! When to love someone means to make love to that someone, then it becomes hard to trust that simple friendship might be more life-giving than having sex.

I find that in our culture most people have given up on the ideal of deep life-giving friendships between women and men.

This despair usually expresses itself, not in a knife to the wrist or in a downed bottle of pills, but in the kind of statement that the young man makes to Cher in the movie *Moonstruck*: "I know this is all wrong! We probably don't love each other and are all wrong for each other and we are going to mess up our lives and our families, but come up to my room this instant and let's go to bed!"

Few things are as healing and life-giving as is friendship between woman and man, man and woman. As God said, "It is not good for the man to be alone!" With Rilke, I believe that, in the end, friendship survives longer than sex and spawns a wider, deeper, more life-giving intimacy.

But it is rare. Deep, intimate, chaste heterosexual friendship is no small achievement. We lack models and are virtual pioneers in this partially uncharted area.

Heterosexual friendships require a delicate balance between caution and risk, between inhibition and daring vulnerability. But they are worth the risk and the effort. When we write our autobiographies, I hope, like Annie Dillard, we can write something like this: "I would give my heart to one oddball after another...and for years on end, and forsook everything else in life, and rightly so, to begin learning with them that unplumbed intimacy that is life's chief joy" (*An American Childhood*).

Emerging From Stone

A powerful and haunting piece of sculpture is Michelangelo's *The Awakening Slave*. It shows a body struggling to emerge from stone, to pull itself free. Part of the body is already clearly formed; the rest is still inchoate, hidden, and imprisoned in stone.

Few images capture as much the feeling of what it means to be human! Born as infants we are helpless, with little self-consciousness, dependent, unable to speak, unable to really know ourselves and others, bound by countless limitations. In the moment of birth we partly emerge from the stone. The rest of our life is a struggle to be born further, to pull ourselves further free.

But, very early, we sense that it is hard. We are so limited in our intelligence, in our energy, in our psyches, in our emotions, in our moral abilities, in our relationships, and in our physical make-up. We push too hard and something breaks!

There is only one place where we do not sense our limits, only one place where we can fly, free of stone—in our dreams. In the kind that we dream in our ideals (not the kind we dream at night) we can truly dance, fly, love perfectly, be totally beyond our own and others limits.

There are no limitations of energy, love, relationships, or emotion in our dreams. There we can pull ourselves completely free from the stone and, then, turn around and look at our actual imprisonment.

Unfortunately too many of us no longer dream. Dreaming is out of fashion. Realism, cynicism, and despair are in vogue. To dream today is to be laughed at, ridiculed, to be regarded as naive, childish, and ultimately as pitiable.

We see this, for example, in the common reaction to anything that is idealistic, romantic, virginal, or contains the type of things we used to write poetry about. Nobody seems to be challenged by these things any more to dream dreams, to push themselves into deeper and more special realms. Mostly these things are met with cynicism and disbelief, coupled with the urge to debunk and with the pitying condescension that we save for the especially naive. Kid's stuff!

I am saddened by this critique. I have seen hopelessness, the lack of dreams, in eighty year olds in bad health, shunted off unwanted, to die in nursing homes because nobody wants them any longer. It is justifiably hard for them to dream!

But when I see, basically, the same hopelessness in gifted, beautiful, richly endowed young people with every practical reason in the world to be dreaming great dreams, I can only be saddened. Despair—and so young. Why?

We have stopped dreaming. We have been sucked in by an unvirginal cynicism of an age that confuses despair with realism. We have stopped struggling and—bottom line—we have despaired that we can ever have a profound relationship, a real romance, genuine community, aesthetic love, or full sexuality.

Belief in them is like belief in Santa Claus and the Easter Bunny. That's for kids! We have settled for what we can have, second best, and are cyncial about any more idealistic realities. Those of us who are married are no longer trying to attain the optimum with our partner. We have settled for some less demanding second best, or are looking elsewhere.

Those of us who are celibate are no longer trying, with all the incredible tension this involves, to love genuinely, yet celibately. Our cynicism has declared that the ideal is impossible and so we become either a sterile old bachelor or maid, or we live a double standard.

All cynicism is despair, pure and simple. All refusal to dream dreams of something beyond is a giving up, a resignation to mediocrity, a self-imposed condemnation to remain partly unborn, in prison. Despair is simply the defeat of our dreams of greatness.

Few things mire us as deeply in the stone as does our refusal to believe in the idea. "There is only one real sin," Doris Lessing once remarked, "and that is calling second best by anything other than what it really is, second best!" Moreover it is important that we do not just dream alone. Dreams need to be shared. What we dream alone remains a dream, what we dream with others becomes a reality! Pain and imprisonment result because people have no one to dream with. No person can cut themselves free of the stone by themselves. We achieve nothing truly in isolation.

We need to dream and to share those dreams: build dream castles in our minds, ideal loves and communities in our hearts. We cannot get fully out of the stone in fact, but we can in desire, in our dreams. They are the chisel we can use to slowly cut away the stone and enable ourselves to emerge to further birth. Everything can be overcome if we dream. Through dreams we see the end of our exile.

Does all this sound like the ravings of an unrealistic dreamer? The naive daydreams and the wishful thinking of a young man out of touch with reality? The rantings of someone with delusions of grandeur?

Perhaps! They are the dreams of a young man, a very idealistic one in fact. And, yes, he has delusions of grandeur! But they are not my dreams. You can read about them in John's Gospel, chapter 17.

Dare to Be One in a Thousand

Recently I was giving a talk to a group of young adults preparing for marriage and was trying to challenge them with the Christian teaching on love and sexuality. They were objecting constantly.

When I had finished speaking a young man stood up and said, "Father, I agree with your principles, in the ideal. But you are totally unrealistic. Do you know what is going on out here? Nobody is living that stuff any more. You'd have to be one person in a thousand to live what you're suggesting. Everyone is living differently now."

I looked at him, sitting beside a young woman whom he obviously loved deeply and hoped to marry, and decided to appeal to his idealism. I asked him, "When you marry that lady beside you, what kind of marriage do you want? One like everyone else's, or one in a thousand?"

"One in a thousand," he answered without hesitation.

"Then," I suggested, "you'd best do what only one in a thousand does. If you do what everyone else does, you will have a marriage like everyone else. If you do what only one in a thousand does, you can have a one-in-a-thousand marriage."

That is not complex theology; it is simple mathematics, but it needs to be said. More and more, as I lecture and write, I am being challenged by people, young and old, who are protesting against idealism. This protest takes many forms. Most commonly it sounds something like this: "Whether certain principles and values are true or false is not so relevant. What is relevant is that virtually everyone has decided to ignore them and live in a different way. Nobody is living like that any more—everyone is living in this way now!"

Implicit in this is that if everyone is living in a certain way, then this way must be right. Values by common denominator. Principles by Gallup poll. Occasionally this critique takes a more cynical bent: "Idealism is naive, for kids. The mature, the realistic do not live with their heads in the clouds. Hence, adjust, update, recognize what is there and accept it; live like everyone else is living."

What an incredible and tragic loss of idealism! Such a philosophy voices despair because the deepest demand of love, Christianity, and of life itself is precisely the challenge to specialness, to what is most ideal. Love, Christianity, and life demand that we take the road less taken, that we be in restless cogitation for a higher eros, that we be one in a thousand.

Our culture, on the other hand, is rejecting this and is swallowing us whole. The current culture is reversing Robert Frost's famous adage and telling us "to take the road more taken." Prophecy is seen as unrealistic, idealism as immature. We are growing ever more dumb. Hence our task today is to be leaven, to be idealistic, and in that way to be prophetic.

Our culture's demand that everyone be like everyone else is not so much malicious as it is despairing. The death of idealism is a child of despair, always. People are content to settle for an attainable second best only when, for whatever reasons (hurt, with a bad self-image and lack of hope) they have given up on ever attaining what is ultimately best.

Today we need prophets. We need people who, when speaking of love, economics, values, sexuality, and aesthetics, are compassionate enough to be empathetic to our real struggles.

In being prophetic in this way, we can show the world that we truly live it because, ultimately, nobody wants a homogenized culture; nobody wants the lowest common denominator within relationships, love, and sexuality; nobody wants to despair that we can feed the hungry and create a more just world; and nobody wants a world that despairingly says: "The best, what's truly special, cannot be reached, so simply settle for what is happening. Do what everyone else is doing; that's good enough!"

It is not good enough. What is truer and deeper inside us knows that there is more and wants more. Philosophies, theologies, and spiritualities that proclaim, "Do what everyone else is doing and that is good enough" break the commandment, that says "Thou shalt not kill!"

In an address in West Germany in 1980, John Paul II called on Christians to be prophets in this sense. Our culture, he stated, tends to declare "human weakness a fundamental principle, and so make it a human right. Christ, on the other hand, taught that a person has above all a right to his or her own greatness."

Thirteen-year-old Anne Frank concurred: That is the difficulty in these times: "Ideals, dreams and cherished hopes rise within us, only to meet the horrible truth and be shattered. It's really a wonder that I haven't dropped my ideals, because they seem so absurd and impossible to carry out. Yet I must uphold my ideals, for perhaps the time will come when I will be able to carry them out" (July 15, 1944, third from last entry in her diary).

May we have the courage to uphold our ideals, even when we cannot fully live them.

Remembering as Surgery

There is a fine line between nostalgia and the longing for lost innocence. The latter is healthy, the former is not. Nostalgia is an unhealthy depression, an adolescent sentimentality that leaves us clinging to the past so as to be unable to enter the present with verve and vitality. In the end it is a mummification, an unnatural embalming of something dead.

For a Christian there is the challenge to move beyond that, to let go, to not cling, to accept death, loss, and corruption in order to be open to accept the new life and new spirit that the present brings.

Unfortunately nostalgia comes upon us looking like the angel of light, with a power to touch our deepest parts in the same way as we are touched by real love and truth. But in the final analysis, like masturbation, it merely deals with something that touches depth. Of itself it is a turning away from reality in favor of fantasy. Not surprisingly it carries with it the appropriate concomitant depression. These words are harsh, but they need to stand as a preamble for what follows.

We all need, occasionally, to make a recessive journey to our origins, to our youth, our innocence, to that place in time and in our hearts, before our sophistication, when we were truly young, simple, and happy. Such a journey refocuses us and gives us a renewed sense of what is truest in us.

But such a journey is not a sentimental voyage into the past in which we recall our youth, its simplicity, and its innocence, and then bring appropriate lessons and guilts to bear upon the present. That would only lead to depression. The recessive journey, rather, is not so much a reexamination of our past as it is an examination of what is truest in us. In the deepest part of our hearts lie our real roots. At the end of that journey we find that our life has not been lost, blown, screwed up beyond hope or irrevocably wounded into melancholy by death, sin, and loss.

The journey to remember, to recall origins, is not a sentimentality; it is a surgery, a cutting away of cancerous overlay to set the heart, in its primal and perennial vitality and innocence, free. I made some such journeys lately. I did some remembering. Partly it was nostalgia, partly surgery.

The recall of myself as a child is both humbling and humiliating; more the former. We were poor and many around an old wooden table in an immigrant district of a rural county. On a farm too small we struggled to learn a new language, to become educated, to do more than just make do, but for years we struggled just to survive.

I am younger than the depression, but I can recall the winter of 1955. We were so poor then. We were always poor. My overriding memory of childhood is of being hungry, not so much for food, but more for a world beyond a small isolated farm, for a life and an experience beyond a world in which there was no hot water on tap and in which there was not even the capability of speaking the language properly or dressing properly.

I felt cursed then by the sense that I was poor. And I was, in some ways, moving about in my patched, hand-me-down clothes, too often smelling of farmyard and barnyard. The shame of poverty hits hardest in the teen years. To step back into that now can still bring flushes of humiliation. To truly recall it, however, brings a healthy humbling coupled with a strength and a sense of richness that nourishes like Elijah's jug.

We were rich in fact, all of us growing up in poverty on those immigrant farms. Our houses and hearts contained all that is important.

Dirty, barefoot, speaking in our multiple accents, we were full of excitement. Our hearts were keen, clear as crystal, eager to learn, and full of appreciation. There was enough love and innocence around.

My life has been blessed with various kinds of riches and successes since then. Through travel, lecturing, teaching, and friendships I have been given the opportunity to experience in reality most of what I dreamed about as a runny-nosed but wide-eyed child. But with the success and experience has come a crippling pseudo-sophistication, an unfreedom, a lack of innocence, a certain fatigue of the spirit, and a fear that can make a recessive journey to my origins an event of depressive nostalgia. The verve, the happiness, the innocence, why are they too often lacking?

Lately I have had to take to dreaming again. It is time, when that happens, to take a recessive journey, to go back to the farm, to recall one's origins. In remembering there is a surgery. When we were little boys and girls our hearts were so eager to learn, our spirits so hungry and welcoming. So much was gift.

Lord, let it all be gift again!

Single Life Offers Opportunities

The refusal of woman is a fault in my chastity...and all my compensations are a desperate and useless expedient to cover this irreparable loss which I have not fully accepted.

I can learn to accept it in the spirit and in love and it will no longer be "irreparable." The cross repairs and transforms it. The tragic chastity which suddenly realizes itself to be mere loss, and the fear that death has won— that one is sterile, useless, hateful. I do not say this is my lot, but in my vow I can see this as an ever-present possibility. (Quoted in J.H. Griffin, *Follow the Ecstasy*)

Those are the words of Thomas Merton as he reflects upon the dangers of not marrying. In sexual inconsummation, be it a deliberately chosen state or one imposed by circumstance, there is always the feeling, seldom far from the surface, that there is something sterile within one's existence.

Merton designated this as "a fault in one's chastity," a fault that can either be tragic or transformed by the cross. I have thought about this a lot, not just as it pertains to persons living a single life in the world.

For many of them life can seem particularly unfair. Society is set up for couples. They are alone. Society has accepted and made a place for consecrated religious. However, singles in the world, while sharing the celibate lot of consecrated religious, share virtually none of their security or advantages.

Moreover, unlike married persons and consecrated religious, singles in the world are rarely given a thriving set of symbols that can provide a symbolic hedge within which to understand their inconsummation. Too often single persons in the world feel they are looking in at life from the outside, that they are abnormal, that they are missing something fundamental in life. Consequently, unlike married persons and consecrated religious, few single persons feel they have positively chosen their state of life. They feel victimized into it. Few single persons feel relaxed, easeful, and accepting of their lot. The feeling, instead, is always that this must be temporary. Rarely can a young single person project his or her future acceptingly to the end and see himself or herself growing old and dying single and happy. Invariably the feeling is this: Something has to happen to change this! I do not choose this! I cannot see myself for the rest of my life like this!

There are immense dangers in these feelings. First there is the danger of simply never fully and joyfully picking up one's life and seeing it as worthwhile, of never choosing to be what one is, of never accepting the spirit that fits the life that one is actually living. As well, there is the danger of panicking and marrying simply because marriage is seen as a panacea and no possibility of real happiness is seen outside it.

Some of these feelings are good. The truth sets us free and so it is not good to pretend pious lies, denial, or spiritualities of espousal with God that do little to placate the emotions, that cannot erase the facts: "It is not good for the man to be alone," the universe works in pairs, the absence of consummation creates a fault in one's chastity that the Creator has condemned.

To be single is to be different, more different than we often dare admit. But it is in the admitting that truth can set us free. However, for that to happen, certain things must be understood and accepted.

Sexuality is a dimension of our self-awareness. We awake to consciousness and feel ourselves, at every level, as cut off, sexed, lonely nomads separated and aching for unity. Celibacy is a fault in our chastity.

However, to be single is not necessarily to be asexual or sterile. Today sometimes the impression is given that sexual union is happiness and no happiness is possible outside that. That is a superficial and dangerous algebra. Sexuality is the drive in us toward connection, community, family, friendship, affection, love, creativity, and generativity. We are happy and whole when these things are in our lives, not on the basis of whether or not we sleep alone. The single celibate life offers its own unique opportunities for achieving these. God never closes one door without opening a few others.

In recognizing that it is easier to find a lover than a friend, we also recognize that human sexuality and generativity are more than biological. Biology is one thing, but there are other ways of being deeply sexual, other ways of getting pregnant and impregnating, other kinds of sexual intimacy, and other ways of being mother and father. There is a mysterious dynamic within separation and community. Sexuality and community function at various levels.

I remember a young man I worked with several years back. He was discerning between religious life and marriage. At one point he commented: "I have always been afraid of being a priest because it will mean dying alone. My father died when I was fifteen and he died in my mother's arms. I have always rejected the celibate state because I want to die like my father died—in a woman's arms.

"However, one day I was meditating on Christ's life and it struck me powerfully that he died alone, loved, but in nobody's arms. He was really alone, though he was powerfully linked to everyone in a different way. It struck me that this could also be a good way to die!"

3

Passion, Love, and Sex

To love a person is to say,
you at least will not die!

Gabriel Marcel

Romance Gives an Inkling of Heaven

A Canadian poet, J. S. Porter, has published a book of poems under the title *The Thomas Merton Poems* (Moonstone Press, 1988). His claim is that Merton might have written these poems had he lived longer. Merton, I suspect, would indeed recognize himself in them.

One poem that particularly caught my eye is without title:

> There's too much of everything
> > books, stars, flowers.
> How can one flower be precious
> > in a bed of thousands?
> How can a book count
> > in a library of millions?
> The universe is a junkyard
> > burnt out meteors, busted up stars
> > planetary cast offs, throwaway galaxies
> > born and buried in an instant
> > repeating, repeating
> Yet something remains
> > the dream of fewness
> > one woman, one man.

There was a time in my life when this poem would have burned holes into me and left me haunted and restless. The dream of fewness/one woman, one man. It still touches the deepest parts of me and triggers a certain ache; but there are now other parts of me that raise questions that were not, until recently, inside me.

Is this dream a dream of the adolescent? Are we longing for a teenage crush? Is it speaking of something more aptly termed obsessional neurosis? Does it refer to something we are meant to outgrow, first fervor, untransformed love? Are we talking here of naive, unrealistic Hollywood daydreams? Are we talking here of a narcissistic longing to find another lonely person with whom to gang-up against genuine community? Are we talking here about a dream of a sick, privatized, selfish life which (as Marxism suggested years ago) hinders the movement toward justice and wider community? Is this a dream for dizzy romance or for what's most precious in God's kingdom?

These questions themselves need questioning. What is their root? Are they the fruit of growing up or are they the fruit of cynicism, tiredness, a fatigued spirit, and a heart that has lost its ideals and is content with second best?

I suspect it is some of both. The dream of fewness can be adolescent and can lead to much useless restlessness and aching. Its pursuit can be counterproductive of community and a hindrance to justice. However, the loss of this dream can also indicate a heart that has lost its most important fire for life and has domesticated its passion.

The dream of fewness comes from our wildest longings and is an ache for a great love. As such, whatever its dysfunctions, it is God's lure pulling us toward our real aim, glory.

Nobody who still believes in the dream of fewness needs the reminder that we "do not live by bread alone," that there is infinitely more to living than the simple sweetening of life. This dream spawns within us a deep and unrelenting restlessness which, perhaps more than anything else, can push us beyond our instinct to settle in, consume, hoard, be secure, and let the amusements and distractions of the good life be somehow enough for us.

To dream the dream of fewness is to know, right within the restless stirring of one's own heart, that one is, as both Scripture and philosophy affirm, fired into life with a madness that comes from the gods and that demands that one attain a great love. It is only when we despair of attaining that great love that we grow embarrassed with romance, with "falling in love," with the dream of fewness, and attempt to tame our longings by subduing them with phrases like naive, adolescent, counterproductive of community, sickly privatized, and obsessional neurosis.

Already a generation ago, C. S. Lewis commented upon this:

> In speaking of this desire...I feel a certain shyness. I am almost committing an indecency. I am trying to rip open the inconsolable secret in each one of you—the secret which hurts so much that you take revenge on it by calling it names like nostalgia and romanticism and adolescence, the secret also which pierces with such sweetness that, when, in very intimate conversation, the mention of it becomes imminent, we grow awkward and affect to laugh at ourselves, the secret we cannot hide and cannot tell.

A friend of mine who was getting married tried to assure me that she knew what she was getting into: "I'm being realistic, Father. This isn't naive passion. I'm not looking for Hollywood romance."

I sent her the poem on the dream of fewness with a note that read something like this: "Enjoy the first fruits of your love, your honeymoon, the dream of fewness. It's one of the better foretastes of heaven given us in this life. The accidents of life, soon enough, deprive us of that. Taste and remember!"

The dream of fewness. Taste and remember. Think of how much happier and mellower and centered beyond the immediate the world would be if everyone had tasted and could remember.

Passion Is God's Fire in Us

Fifty years ago T.S. Eliot predicted the death of passion, poetry, fidelity, and historical consciousness. Today, tragically, that prediction is coming true.

As Christians we need to recognize that fact and respond, in order to defend passion and challenge people to it. That sounds strange and it is. Passion has, at least so it seems, always been distrusted in religious circles and extolled in secular ones. Indeed the secular world tended to claim passion as its own, as something irreligious, as the very force that is rebellious against religion and that, if responded to, frees one from the shackles of religion.

Preachers, priests, spiritual writers, and church leaders tended to help this idea along. The church, it seemed, was forever lashing out against passion, pointing out its dangers and forbidding people to allow themselves to feel and enjoy the full emotional, psychological, and instinctual force of their eros. Passion was made to seem at odds with religion.

How wrong we were! And how wrong the secular world has discovered itself to be! There has been a strange and ironic reversal.

Today the secular world is trying to rid itself of all passion and the church is suddenly, much to its own surprise, finding itself in the novel position of having to defend passion. Why this turn of events? Because the secular world has discovered passion to be a very inconvenient thing. Passion, romance, poetry, aesthetics—all these things challenge infidelity.

Thus our culture has begun to classify passion as it classifies other religious things, namely, as something medieval, the product of naivety, as something from which people need to be freed. How deliciously ironic! The very force that it had so long claimed as uniquely its own, trumpeted as its victory, has, when given rein, proved to be an inconvenient embarrassment. Passion, in the end, is only for religious persons. Why? Because our world exalts a false kind of freedom. In our society we're exhorted to hang loose, to run from involvement, to run away from anything that might tie us down. We are invited to live as "free spirits," soaring, fulfilled, unencumbered. Passion and romance spell death for that kind of freedom. Passion means involvement, attachment, surrender, a loss of control and freedom, commitment. If sustained, it means fidelity.

For this reason it is no accident that, for the most part, secular wisdom today considers passion in the same way as it considers religion—kid's stuff, for the naive. Today passion and romance are seen as things we need therapy from. In his astute and very disturbing book, *The Triumph of the Therapeutic*, Philip Rieff, who is no friend of religion, points out that in our present culture passion and romance are "archaic and dispensable." They are what Freud calls "erotic illusions" and, as Rieff goes on to say, it is time we stopped organizing our personalities and our communities around them.

Love and hatred, the products of passion, are, in his words, obsolete as organizing modes of personality. In a culture of contacts and infidelity, passion and romance are experienced as tyranny. Bottom line: today romantic love is considered a neurosis, a sickness or, at best, something for the very young or very naive, a hangover from former ages, as is religion.

For this reason it is important that Christians and the Christian churches rush to the defense of passion and romance. They are part of God's fire in us, a great gift, to be channeled prudently, it is true, but nonetheless to be ever perceived precisely as a gift from God. Today they are badly needed. They challenge infidelity.

When T.S. Eliot predicted the death of poetry, passion, fidelity, and historical consciousness, it is no accident that he placed all of these together. They flow from each other. Passion and poetry, when released and given, bond us to each other and to history in a way that makes infidelity and false freedom much more difficult. In a culture characterized by flightiness, lack of commitment, hanging loose, infidelity, cynicism, and programmed boredom, we need fire, passion, and romance. They perhaps more than anything else can help turn the tide and become the vaccine that immunizes us against the infectious bacteria set loose by the cynicism and infidelity of our age.

The fire of passion comes from God. Eros is at the root of human soul and body. In the Hasidic tradition there is a famous parable about a man who wanted to be a blacksmith. So he bought a hammer, an anvil, and bellows. But he could not bend any iron. There was no flame, no heat in his forge. He had everything except the thing he most needed— the spark, the fire, the heat that makes things malleable.

In a world in which fidelity and historical consciousness are dying and being replaced by infidelity and programmed boredom, in a world in which true romance and true sexuality are being replaced by schizophrenic sex and pornography, we need fire in the forge, passion and romance. Christians need to arise in the defence of eros.

Sexuality Is More Than Sex

As a Catholic priest I am seldom taken seriously when I speak or write about sex. Invariably the reaction is: "What can you know about it? You don't have sex!"

I welcome that comment because it betrays the very attitude toward sex that I want to challenge, namely, it identifies sexuality with having sex.

That is dangerously false and few things are as bad for us emotionally as that idea. Yet popularized Freudianism has given us this idea. It has made us believe that real love and friendship, at least of the heterosexual variety, depend upon having sexual relationships. In brief it has made us believe that we cannot be whole without sex. Without sex, it is believed, we will end up sterile, dried up old maids, "that way." Without sex our friendships and loves will be Platonic, anemic, and unreal.

Conncomitantly we nurse the idea that having sex is a panacea for all loneliness and emotional frustration. Sexology is too commonly a substitute for soteriology, meaning that happiness and sadness are identified with a fulfilling sexual relationship or its absence.

Because of this we suffer emotionally. When sexuality is synonymous with having sex, then, save brief moments, we live in much frustration and restless dissatisfaction. For all kinds of reasons we cannot sleep with everyone we feel drawn to and since friendship and love have become too much linked to sex we are constantly torn between infidelity and frustration. The tragedy is not just that there is so much sexual and emotional infidelity around, but that, because of this, there is so little heterosexual friendship and love around (even within marriage).

It is no accident that in our culture it is easier to find a lover than a friend, just as it is no accident that, in our culture, virginity, celibacy, chastity within deep friendships and periodic abstinence within marriage are considered to be unrealistic or even positively harmful. Yet our deepest hungers and longings are for heterosexual relations beyond having sex. The ache is for men and women to come together as more than lovers.

This is not surprising. Sexuality is a huge thing. Our aches are multifarious. The word sex comes from the Latin *secare*, literally, to cut off or divide from. We experience ourselves, at all levels, precisely as sexed, as cut off, divided from, unwhole. We ache for consummation, for a reuniting with some wholeness. For this reason sexuality is always more than simply having sex. It is a dimension of our self-awareness. It is our eros, that irrepressible demand within us that we love and that energy within us that enables us to love. Through it we break out of the shells of our own egos and narcissism. Through it we seek contact, communication, wholeness, community, and creativity. Through sexuality we are driven and drawn beyond ourselves.

The sense of being sexed, cut off, is as present in us as our heartbeat. It permeates every level of our personalities and colors all of our relationships.

We are charged with sex. Physically, psychologically, spiritually, emotionally, intellectually, and aesthetically we ache for union with something beyond ourselves. Maleness aches for femaleness, femaleness for the male. Sex colors all.

Yet having sex is merely one specific expression of our sexuality. It is simply one part, albeit a poignant one, of a much larger reality we call sexuality. It is our contemporary inability to understand this that lies at the root of our obsession with sex. Around us, like an infectious virus, floats the idea that our personalities will expand or shrink depending on whether we are having satisfying sex or not.

However, if sexuality is the drive for community, family, friendship, love, and creativity, then whether we sleep alone or not is not so important. Community, family, friendship, and creativity are. We can live with sex or without it, but we cannot live without community, family, friendship, and creativity. Our lives become warmer, more meaningful, and more whole when these are there.

Conversely we grow colder and become bitter, sterile, and dried up when they are absent. Our irrepressible longing is for community, family, friendship, and creativity. Sexuality is the hunger and energy for them.

Having sex must always be understood within this context. It can help or harm. It helps when it fosters community, family, friendship, and creativity. It harms when it blocks them. Given the contours of our personalities and our social lives, it appears impossible that, outside a relationship of love, permanent commitment, and marriage, having sex can foster community, family, and friendship. Experience tends to bear this out. Severing the tie between sex and marriage has not translated into more friendship, more community, more family, and more love. We are lonelier than ever.

There is sex of the groin and sex of the heart. The former is full of dissatisfaction, exploitation, superficiality, schizophrenia, and ultimately boredom (since, as W.H. Auden remarks, "All of us know the few things man as a mammal can do"). The latter is full of friendship, romance, and passion. It is sex of the heart that cures loneliness and creates family, community, and friendship.

We need, again, to learn the differences between sexuality and having sex.

No Salvation in Sexology

A nun I know was traveling one day by air and found herself
engaged in a conversation with a lively young man. He had a
myriad of questions, many concerning celibacy. At a certain
point he remarked, "Looking at you, what intrigues me is that
you are obviously a person who has a zest for life. Now think,
Sister, how much richer your life could be if you also had sex!"

The nun simply replied, "Looking at you, what intrigues me
is that you are obviously a person who is sincere and is searching for love. Love and sex aren't always the same thing. Now
think how much richer your life could be if you understood
that!"

This incident can help us understand why Christ chose to
incarnate his sexuality in the manner that he did, namely, as
virgin.

By living and loving as virgin, Christ was not in any way
trying to teach—as has sometimes been taught in the past—
that consecrated celibacy is superior to marriage or that there
is something within sexual relations that works against the
spiritual life. Rather, that the kingdom of God is more about
the human heart than it is about the human groin.

Within Christ's perspective, the kingdom of God is about
love, the non-exploitive meeting of human hearts. It consists of
God and all persons of sincere will coming together in an all-
in-one-heart-and-flesh community of life within which hearts
are bonded in friendship, love, celebration, and playfulness.

Sex has a place within that, a beautiful and intensely poignant place. But it is not the kingdom, and to be the beautiful
gift it was created to be it must always be linked to a chaste
and permanent meeting of human hearts. It may never just be,
as poet Margaret Atwood puts it, "a dentistry, the slick filling

of aches and cavities." Few messages are as urgently needed by our age as this challenge from Jesus to properly sort through the relationship between love and sex. We are a society that has all but turned sexology into a doctrine of salvation.

The classical language of salvation (which is the language of love)—"paying the price of sin," "giving until crucifixion," "suffering unto death"—has, for the largest part, been replaced by the language of sex. Love and salvation are talked about more in the language of Masters and Johnson than they are in the language of Christ. Accordingly, for too many of us, love and salvation are seen more as the temporary mating of human bodies than as the permanent meeting of human hearts.

The price we pay for this is loneliness. It is no mere accident that we are probably the loneliest society in the recorded history of humankind. We are also probably the most sexually active. Somehow, the increase in sexual activity has not translated itself into an alleviation of loneliness and restlessness. For all our sexual freedom and sophistication, we are caught up ever more deeply in restless chaos.

There is salvation in love alone. There is no justification in sex alone. The algebra of Christ's virginity is that, among other things, friendship and love, celebration and community, happiness and the kingdom lie in the coming together of hearts. Sexuality contributes to the building up and the consummation of this community of hearts only when it helps lead to the joy and order that come from fidelity and chastity.

As Christians, therefore, we must incarnate our sexuality into the world in such a way that it constantly shows that love and the heart are the central realities of life and the kingdom.

We do this not by attempting to be asexual, or by setting the enjoyment of sex against the spiritual life, but rather by attempting to be sexual in the proper sense—namely, in the way that Christ was. This can be done whether we are celibate or married.

If we are celibate and chaste, and yet are persons who are interpersonally unfearful, clearly sexual, and warmly human, then we cannot help but challenge an age which, for all its searching, lives in loneliness and pain. Celibacy, if properly lived, can be an important way to keep alive, visible, and in the flesh that part of the incarnation which tells us that, when one is speaking of love, the human heart is the central organ. Marriage, if properly lived out, is also excellently suited to teach this. Married persons imitate and help keep incarnate Christ's sexuality just as celibates do. Christ's virginity was not intended to set the joys of sex against the spiritual life. Sexually consummated love, if it is respectful, esthetic, and linked to fidelity, is also a visible, enfleshed prolongation of the incarnation.

Since married love puts sexuality and love into their proper relationship, it visibly prolongs and transubstantiates Christ's sexuality. It not only helps keep incarnate the life-creating power of sexuality, but it challenges powerfully the misconstrued notion that suggests that sex, disembodied from chastity and commitment, can in any way play a meaningful role in bringing final happiness and fulfillment into human life—or indeed be of any use in the building up and consummation of God's kingdom.

How much richer our lives could be if we understood that!

Three Phases of Fantasy

We have always been taught that it is a bad thing to fantasize about sex, to have "bad thoughts." That may be true, but it is virtually impossible and perhaps unhealthy not to think about sex. We are so incurably sexual.

We ache for wholeness and, as we ache, we fantasize about that union which can end our aloneness. Our very condition spawns perpetual sexual temptations. That comes from God and is good. Sex is a powerful, huge thing. Like breathing, it is part and parcel of being alive, and like breathing it is necessary for life. It is not one isolated part of ourselves. Sex is co-extensive with our personalities in that it is a dimension of our self-awareness. It is the way we seek contact, community, and unity beyond ourselves and our separate egos. It is an energy, a power for loving, a merciless tension that pushes us outwards.

As such it affects our whole being. All of our relationships and actions are sexually colored, tainted if you will, in some way. We do little, perhaps nothing, that is not affected, however inchoately, by the fact that we are cut off, divided, sexed.

But to say that sexuality seeps through into nearly all we think and do need not be a shameful confession; it can be a statement of health. Hence, sexual fantasizing can also be an indication of health rather than automatically a sign of selfishness and perversion. But this needs considerable nuance: Our sexuality is developmental and so too should be its attendant fantasies. What follows is an outline of certain discernible phases of sexual maturation and their consequences for sexual fantasizing. This schema is developed for the male sexual cycle but, with certain variations, is equally true for women.

The adolescent phase of sexuality begins with puberty and

can last into the late twenties. At this stage, sexuality is predominantly genital. It can be indiscriminate in that its temptations and at times its actions can be frighteningly unmonogamous. It tends to be centered very much on pleasure, physical and emotional. One's fantasy life generally follows suit. Bad thoughts during this time are generally pretty bad, namely, thoughts that are precisely genitally focused, that dwell on the bodily pleasures of sex.

But this phase normally gives way, during the mid to late twenties, or in some cases earlier, to a sexuality that yearns much more for intimacy than for sheer sexual pleasure or indiscriminate sexual union. In this second stage sexuality becomes less raw, more discriminate, more romantic. The fantasy of intimacy, of embrace, replaces cruder versions. At this stage sexual feelings widen to take in more aspects of the person. At this stage too it begins to become more difficult to consider sexual fantasies simply as bad thoughts. Somehow the fantasy of embrace suggests more goodness and wholeness than it suggests dirtiness and evil, unless of course it does not respect other persons' privacy, chastity, marriages, and commitments.

But sexuality has yet a further phase. By one's mid to late thirties the issues of procreation, children, and wider community begin to take center stage. Sexuality at every level, body, mind, emotions, psyche, spirit, begins to demand that we give birth to something or, like Jephthah's daughter, it begins to mourn and bewail its virginity. Sexual union, even intimacy with some loved one, however deep and true, is no longer enough. Our sexuality now hungers beyond that. Our sexual energies, our erotic tensions, must now be poured out for a wider community. At this point in life all sexual pleasure and sexual intimacy becomes unhealthily narcissistic if it does not accept this.

And this is also true for our life of fantasy. As our sexuality widens and begins to be focused more on giving birth and on community, so too must our concomitant fantasies.

At this stage of our lives, I dare submit, we must cultivate sexual thoughts, but they must be fantasies of how we can pour our sexuality, the tension and energy inside us that is felt in our sense of being cut off and divided, into nurturing life, into new ways of producing life, into new ways of impregnating and being impregnated so as to help bring about new birth and new community.

We will always fantasize and we will always fantasize sexually. To be human is to have a fertile mind and imagination. To be sensitive is to have fertile feelings and fertile fantasies. For better and for worse we are stuck with our "bad thoughts." When are they a share in God's hunger for a kingdom, something to be fostered, and when are they bad thoughts, something to be confessed? When are they healthy and when are they unhealthy? Perhaps there are no clear answers to those questions.

However, even in a world in which the huge issues of social morality such as starvation, social injustice, abortion, and the threat of nuclear war tend to make speculation on issues of private morality seem petty, these are worthwhile and ultimately important questions.

4

The Fire in One's Eyes: Losing and Recovering Innocence

There comes an hour in the afternoon when the child is tired of pretending; when he is weary of being a robber or an Indian. It is then that he torments the cat. There comes a time in the routine of an ordered civilization when [a person] is tired of playing at mythology and pretending that a tree is a maiden or that the moon made love to a man. The effect of staleness is the same everywhere; it is seen in all our drug-taking and dram-drinking and in every form of the tendency to increase the dose. [People] seek stranger sins or more startling obscenities as stimulants to their jaded senses....They try to stab their nerves to life, as if it were with the knives of the priests of Baal. They are walking in their sleep and try to wake themselves with nightmares.

G.K. Chesterton

The Real Loss of Virginity

Some years ago, while giving a retreat, a woman came to me for confession. Her confession was long and sincere. However, that sincerity and genuine contrition was constantly punctured by a cyncism, sarcasm, and a background experience that caused her to be constantly questioning whether she wanted to be sincere and contrite. She was very bright and very experienced. In virtually every sense of the word, she had been around. She was also very unhappy.

When we had finished she asked what I felt she needed to do. I suggested she should undergo a long and intensive process of "revirginization." It was a suggestion that mildly shocked her, but it was what she really needed. Though young, she had been almost everywhere, done almost everything, and had, in a way of speaking, sophisticated herself into a huge unhappiness. There was not a childlike bone in her body, nor a childlike thought in her heart. She had lost most of her virginity.

That prescriptive counsel I gave her, revirginization, is a counsel that I judge more and more needs to be given to all of us and to our age in general. We are horribly unvirginal persons.

What is meant here?

Virginity is, in its deepest sense, not so much a past sexual history as a present attitude. Whether one is a virgin or not has less to do with his or her past sexual experiences as it has to do with the posture with which he or she meets reality. What is the posture of virginity? It is comprised of three compenetrating elements.

First, virginity is the posture of a child before reality. A child has a very primitive, virginal spirit. In a child's heart and mind, and in a virgin's, there is a sense of newness, of experiencing for the first time. There is also a capacity to be surprised. There is no illusion of familiarity and there is a natural "fear of God," love's fear, the fear that is the beginning of wisdom. Because of this, there is in the child or the virgin a sense of mystery, a sense that some things are sacred, untouchable, beyond manipulation.

Secondly, virginity is living in a certain inconsummation, living with a desire for experience that is not fully satiated. To be a virgin is to live in tension, unfulfilled, longing, waiting for a time in the future when one will be fulfilled. The virgin does not prematurely enter the marriage bed. This is true not just in the area of sexuality, but in all of life.

Finally, virginity is living in such a way that there are certain areas of our personality and life that are revered and sacred and that are then shared only within a context which fully respects that sacredness. For a virgin there is a certain chastity in experiencing, in all areas of life including the sexual.

Virginity opposes itself to promiscuity of all kinds. The virgin knows that the human heart, temple of the Holy Spirit that it is, is not cheap. As a precious gift it may only be trustfully given.

This posture, virginity, is natural in a child. However, here it is dependent upon certain factors that are themselves natural in children, namely, ignorance, lack of experience, superstition, lack of opportunity, natural naivety, and a lack of criticalness and practicalness.

As we grow older, as our critical faculties sharpen and as we experience more, we naturally lose much of our virginity. Partly this is necessary, natural, and healthy—to be adult and naive is not an ideal.

However, partially this loss of virginity is unnecessary and unhealthy. As was the case with the woman described above, partly the loss of virginity is the result of giving in to the urge to experience indiscriminately, of stripping reality unduly of too many of its sacral dimensions, of illicitly breaking taboos (including sexual ones), and of letting impatience and despair drive us beyond chastity.

When this happens, and to a greater or lesser extent it happens in each of our lives, we develop a false familiarity with life and begin to live under the illusion of familiarity. This is the real loss of virginity, living in an unhealthy familiarity with life, others, sex. In this state, all real love, real romance, and all aesthetics in love die. Ultimately the loss of virginity is characterized by a sophisticated unhappiness, an unchildlikeness which, while miserable, refuses to admit its own misery and its cause. That is one of the qualities of being in hell, to be miserable and to refuse to admit it.

With that comes a proclivity for the perverse. Why? Because as Chesterton so aptly puts it: "There comes an hour in the afternoon when the child is tired of pretending; when he is weary of being a robber or an Indian. It is then that he torments the cat."

Lately, as a culture, we have taken to tormenting the cat! How do we wake ourselves from the nightmare?

Saying Yes to Santa Claus

If you ask a naive child: "Do you believe in Santa Claus?" he replies "Yes!" If you ask a bright child the same question, this child replies, "No!" However, if you ask an even brighter child he replies, "Yes!"

I have described our need for "revirginization," our need again to say yes to the question of Santa Claus. But how do we revirginize? How do we move toward a second naivety? We do it by touching the nerve of novelty, by purging ourselves of the illusion of familiarity. We must, as Chesterton put it, "learn to look at things familiar until they look unfamiliar again." We do this by making a deliberate and conscious effort to assume the posture of a child before reality. We must work at regaining the primal spirit, a sense of wonder, the sense that reality is rich and full of mystery, that we do not yet understand, and that we must read chastely, carefully, and discriminately, respecting reality's contours and taboos.

Concomitant with this effort comes the deliberate and conscious attempt at purging ourselves of all traces of cynicism, contempt, and all attitudes that identify mystery with ignorance, taboo with superstition, and romance and ideals with naivety. It also entails the willingness to put off gratification, to live in tension, to accept being unfulfilled. It entails, in every sense of the term, refusing to sleep with the bride before the wedding night. We revirginize by learning to wait—sexually, economically, emotionally, spiritually.

Finally, revirginization and coming to second naivety involves recovering again a certain chastity in experiencing. It involves recovering and respecting the sense that we ourselves and the reality around us are full of sacredness. Perhaps the process of revirginization may best be described by two metaphors.

The image of weather revirginizing a geographical terrain: Imagine a geographical terrain that has been ravaged by natural disaster and despoiled by human beings. Its waters are dirty and polluted, its vegetation is dead, and its natural beauty is destroyed.

However, given time and weather—the sun, the rains, the winds, the storms, the frost, and snow—it, in a manner of speaking, revirginizes. Its waters again grow clear and pure, its vegetation returns to life, and eventually its natural beauty returns. In a manner of speaking, its chastity returns, making it again "virgin territory."

So too with our hearts and minds: As soon as we stop despoiling them through the illusion of familiarity and indiscriminate experience, they too regain gradually their virginity and begin again to blush in the wonder of knowing and loving. A chastity in knowing and loving returns.

Secondly, the image of foetal darkness: Imagine the gestation process of a human being in the womb. The process begins with a mere egg, a cellular speck that is being gestated, formed, cared for, shaped by things around it, and nourished by a reality infinitely larger than itself. The process takes place in darkness, in a dark peace. Eventually the child has grown sufficiently and emerges for the first time.

The sheer overwhelmingness of the mystery of reality is so strong that it takes years for the senses and mind to harden sufficiently for the child to even begin to understand. Initially the child simply looks and wonders.

So with other processes of coming to second naivety, of revirginizing. We must truly be born again. We must, metaphorically speaking, make a recessive journey, a voyage to the sources, to the foetal darkness of the womb to be reduced to a mere egg, to be gestated anew in darkness (in the darkness of an understanding that understands more by not understanding than by understanding) so that we can again open our eyes to a new awareness that is so wild, so startling, so agnostic, and so overpowering that we are unable to name and number, but are reduced, as it were, to having to ponder and to wonder.

G.K. Chesterton expressed this beautifully in *A Second Childhood:*

> When all my days are ending
> And I have no song to sing,
> I think I shall not be too old
> To stare at everything;
> As I stared once at a nursery door
> Or a tall tree and a swing...

May we never grow too old, too sophisticated, too unchildlike, too unvirginal to stare at everything as we "stared once at a nursery door."

Don't Kill Santa Claus Too Soon

In his best-selling book, *The Closing of the American Mind,* Allan Bloom describes a contemporary professor who sees his task as that of setting people free by breaking taboos:

> He reminded me of the little boy who gravely informed me when I was four that there was no Santa Claus, who wanted me to bathe in the brilliant light of truth....My informant about Santa Claus was just showing off, proving his superiority to me....Think of all we learn about the world from people's belief in Santa Clauses, and all we learn about the soul from those who believe in them. By contrast, merely methodological excision from the soul of the imagination (which lets us believe in this kind of thing) does not promote knowledge of the soul, it only lobotomizes it, cripples its powers.

The breaking of taboos, the death of an innocence, however naive, what does this do to the human soul? I was raised in a time when there was an emphasis on chastity. There were a lot of taboos. Many things were not permitted and among many of the important things that were, dating, friendship, marriage, sex, there was a certain protocol that had to be observed: a certain caution, a waiting, a string of taboos, and a proper way in which a thing was to be accomplished. We called it chastity. Not everyone was chaste, of course, but the ideal was basically agreed upon.

Today this has changed. Far from being thought of as positive, as the key to all experience, chastity is associated with being inhibited, repressed, timid, and naive. The push is to break taboos, to experience more things and to experience them earlier.

Few persons, I am sure, would deny this. But many, I suspect, will deny that a lot of the emotional chaos, meaninglessness, and deep despair that is ungluing the Western psyche comes, in the end, from a lack of chastity. Let me explain.

The biggest crisis within our culture is not economic, but psychic. Emotional unrest, deep dis-ease, sexual pathos, the sense of loss, of meaninglessness, of death—these are the deep cancers in Western society. Human goodness remains and God's unconditional love will, ultimately, wash all things clean. But if our souls are not going to the devil they certainly are dying to youth, innocence, enthusiasm, and passion. As Bloom puts it in his book, our eros has gone lame.

Even as we grow emotionally more chaotic and more deeply restless, the eros of our youth and the enthusiasm for true sexuality are dead. We are no longer fired into life by a madness that comes from our incompleteness and lets us believe that we can recover our wholeness through the embrace of another, the perpetuity of our seed, and the contemplation of God.

Instead we are tired, erotically fatigued, lame. We have already been there! We have had a look! There is a deadness within the Western soul. How does this link to chastity, or lack of it?

Already a generation ago, Albert Camus, an atheistic writer, commented, "Chastity alone is connected with personal progress. There is a time when moving beyond it is a victory—when it is released from its moral imperatives. But this quickly becomes a defeat afterwards" (quoted in P. Rieff, _The Triumph of the Therapeutic_).

What Camus is suggesting is that the feeling of emotional despair that is so pervasive in our culture is a result of a lack of chastity. To understand this, however, we need better to understand what chastity is.

Chastity is normally defined as something to do with sex, namely, a certain innocence, purity, discipline, or even celibacy regarding sex. This is too narrow. Chastity is, first, not primarily a sexual concept. It has to do with the limits and appropriateness of all experiencing, sexual experience included.

To be chaste means to experience things, all things, respectfully and to drink them in only when we are ready for them. We break chastity when we experience anything irreverently or prematurely. This is what violates either another's or our own growth. It is the lack of chastity in experiencing, irreverence and prematurity, that lobotomizes the soul.

Experience can be good or bad. It can help glue the psyche together or tear it apart. It can produce joy or chaos. Travel, study, achievement, sex, exposure to newness, the breaking of taboos, all can be good if experienced reverently and at their proper time.

Conversely they can tear the soul apart (even when they are not wrong in themselves) when they are not drunk in chastely, that is, at a pace that respects fully both others' and our own growth. Always look carefully at any taboo. Always link learning to integration, epistemology to morality, experience to chastity. There is much danger in killing Santa Claus too soon.

Staring Chaos in the Face

We live in pain and division. In the world, in the church, and within ourselves, there is much anger, hatred, and bitterness. It seems even harder to live at peace with each other, to be calm, to have simple joy within our lives and not to alienate someone just by being.

Within ourselves, despite the fact that we have virtually every practical reason to be happy—friends, health, material affluence—we experience anger, jealousy, and woundedness. Seldom are we satisfied. Seldom are we truly free of bitterness, anger, and feelings of being slighted and overlooked. Very seldom are we fully at peace with life and with others.

Beyond this, we live in a world that is full of painful division. It has its own wounds. Poverty, social injustice, the in-equality of men and women, racism, abortion, sexual exploitation, narcissistic yuppies, untrustworthy political leaders, and simply millions of persons caught up in excessive self-interest.

It is hard for us, as adults in our world, to simply love, be understanding, and be at peace with others and with life. We are wounded, within and without. The temptation is toward bitterness, anger, withdrawal, and paranoia. That is the road to hell because bitterness is hell.

What is needed to stop our slide toward this is reconciliation at every level. What is reconciliation? It is a reality that admits many levels.

Here I want to speak of reconciliation as personal healing, as a coming inside of ourselves to a new wholeness and a renewed sense of childlike joy. Reconciliation, at this level, involves many things. First it involves the recognition of our woundedness, our neuroses, our bitterness, our narcissism and narrow loyalties, and simply, our lack of joy.

Just as for an alcoholic there can be no real change before there is the basic admittance of the conditions of helplessness and need, so too in our struggle to come to personal healing. There can be no healing until we admit sickness. And we are ill: compulsive, angry, competitive, bitter, narcissistic, cynical, humorless, paranoid, self-pitying, jealous, sombre, and joyless.

The roots of this woundedness stretch deep into our past, and beyond our past into the history of the world. We are not just part of the chain of life, but are likewise part of a chain of neuroses and wounds that stretch back, ultimately, to Adam and Eve.

We can sometimes point to certain events and persons that have hurt us deeply and blame much of our pain on them. However, these events and persons themselves point still further back to distant events and persons that wounded them.

There was some original sin—and life has not been harmonious, not seemed fair, ever since. Reconciliation begins when we truly admit this. So long as we pretend otherwise, it is not even meaningful to use the word. When we claim our woundedness, however, we are brought face to face with our own helplessness, our need, our need for God.

Then, as Henri Nouwen puts it, our hearts "become the place where the tears of God and the tears of God's children can merge and become tears of hope" (*Love in a Fearful Land*, 1986).

The first step in real reconciliation is the tearful acknowledgment of our woundedness, our helplessness, our sin. In this admission is a painful dying and a joyous rebirth.

Ashes make the best fertilizer. Tears wash away sin. Honesty induces the labor that gives birth to conversion.

When we cry honest tears, we are flooded with the desire to pray, to forgive, to serve others, to build a just social order, to live more moral lives, to love beyond resentment and bitterness. That is the movement toward reconciliation and joy.

Why? Because searing honesty brings us face to face with our own woundedness and helplessness; our helplessness, in turn, brings us face to face with a redeeming God. In that encounter, we learn that we are loved sinners. Gratitude is born. A genuine sanctity follows.

Novelist Iris Murdoch states that to be a saint is nothing less than to be armed and vitalized by gratitude. To rid ourselves of resentment, bitterness, jealousy, and paranoia requires a powerful fire. Only the gratitude that flows from knowing that we are loved, loved despite wound and sin, is a large enough flame to burn wound from our lives.

The rest follows: When we are vitalized by gratitude we will automatically move toward deeper prayer, wider loyalties, and a more embracing heart.

Reconciliation begins when we stare our chaos in the face. In that, we will be brought face to face with our helplessness and our need for God. Prayer will then begin, crying out from the very depths of our being. We will be laid bare and will realize that we are loved sinners, in solidarity with other loved sinners like ourselves. Gratitude, reconciliation, and healing will follow.

The Value of Fasting and Feasting

We celebrate feasts differently than we used to. Formerly there was generally a long fast leading up to a feast, and a joyous celebration afterwards. Today, usually, there is a long celebration leading up to the feast, and a fast afterwards.

The way we celebrate Christmas exemplifies this. Nearly two months before the actual day, we begin to celebrate. The parties start, the decorations and lights go up, the cards go out, and the Christmas music begins to play.

When Christmas Day finally arrives we are already satiated with the specialness of the season, tired, oversaturated with celebration, and ready to move on. By then we are ready to go back to ordinary life and even to do some fasting...having had enough of turkey dinners! The Christmas season used to last until February. Now, realistically, it is over on December 25.

This is a curious reversal. Traditionally the build-up was always toward a feast, celebration came after. Today the feast is first, the fast comes after. Why is this? And, are we the better or the worse for reversing the fast/feast cycle?

A colleague of mine commented that our society knows how to anticipate an event, but not how to sustain it. That is only partially true. The real issue is not so much that we do not know how to sustain something, we do not know precisely how to anticipate something. We confuse anticipation with celebration itself.

One of our weaknesses today is that we find it hard to live in the face of any anticipation, inconsummation, or unfulfilled tension without moving swiftly to resolve it. Longing and fasting are not our strong points. Because we cannot build properly toward a feast, we cannot celebrate properly either.

Celebration is an organic process. To feast, one must first

fast; to come to consummation, one must first live in chastity; and to taste specialness one must first have a sense of what is ordinary. When fasting, inconsummation, and the dour rhythm of the ordinary are short-circuited, then fatigue of the spirit, boredom, and disappointment replace celebration. We are left with the empty feeling that says, "All this hype, for this!" Something can only be sublime if, first of all, there is some sublimation.

I am old enough to have known another time. Like our own, this time too had its faults, but it also had its strengths. One of these strengths was its belief, a lived belief, that feasting depends upon prior fasting, that the sublime depends upon a prerequisite sublimation.

I have vivid memories of the Advents and Lents of my childhood. How strict those times were! They were seasons of fast and renunciation: no weddings, no dances, fewer parties, fewer drinks, fewer desserts, and generally less of everything that constitutes specialness and celebration. Churches were draped in purple and statues covered. The colors were dark and the mood penitential; but the feasts that followed, Easter and Christmas, were oh, so special!

Perhaps I am waxing nostalgic; after all, I was young then, naive and deprived, and thus able to meet Christmas and Easter, and other celebrations, with a fresher spirit. That may be, but the specialness that surrounded feasts has died for another, more important reason: We do not anticipate them properly any more.

We short-circuit fasting, inconsummation, and the prerequisite longing. Simply put, how can Christmas be special when we arrive at December 25th exhausted from weeks of Christmas parties? How can Easter be special when we treat Lent just as we treat any other season? How indeed can anything be sublime when we have all but lost our capacity for sublimation?

Celebration, as mentioned earlier, is an organic process. It is created by a dynamic interplay between anticipation and fulfillment, longing and inconsummation, ordinary and special, work and play. Life, love, and sexuality must be celebrated within that fast/feast rhythm. Seasons of play must follow seasons of work, seasons of consummation are contingent upon seasons of longing, and seasons of intimacy can only grow out of seasons of solitude.

Presence depends upon absence, intimacy upon solitude, play upon work. Even God rested only after working for six days!

Today the absence of genuine specialness and enjoyment within our lives is due largely to the breakdown of this rhythm. In a word, Christmas is no longer special because we have celebrated it during Advent, weddings are no longer special because we have already slept with the bride, and experiences of all kinds are often flat, boring, and unable to excite us because we had them prematurely.

Premature experience is bad precisely because it is premature. To celebrate Christmas during Advent, to celebrate Easter without fasting, to short-circuit longing in any area, is, like sleeping with the bride before the wedding, a fault in chastity. All premature experience has the effect of draining us of great enthusiasm and great expectations (which can only be built up through sublimation, tension, and painful waiting).

5

Prayer and the Monasticism of Daily Life

It takes only a slight shift of emphasis, and the point of aloneness in dynamic stillness becomes the point of consummate union.

David Steindl-Rast

The Monasticism of Daily Life

David Steindl-Rast has commented that leisure is not the privilege of those who have time, but rather the virtue of those who give to each instant of life the time it deserves. That is a valuable insight, especially today when everywhere life seems dominated by the constraints of time. Always, it seems, there is not enough time. Our lives are dominated by pressure, the rat race, demands that are all-absorbing. The factory has to run and, by the time that is taken care of, there is no time or energy for anything else.

And we are conscious of our pathological busyness. We know that life is passing us by and we are so preoccupied with the business of making a living and the duties of family and community that only rarely is there any time to actually live. It seems that there is never any unpressured time, unhurried time, undesignated time, leisure time, time to smell the flowers, simply to luxuriate in being alive. We lament about this over our coffee, but are unable effectively to change anything.

Is there something frighteningly wrong with our lives? Is there a need to drastically change our lifestyles?

Perhaps. Obviously in our lives there is too little family time. But we are also compounding our problem through misunderstanding. Philosophies of "taking time to smell the flowers" have sometimes led us to understand leisure precisely as the privilege of the rich and unoccupied. What Steindl-Rast challenges us to do is to understand time correctly.

Time is a gift. When T.S. Eliot says, "Time, not our time," he is pointing out that there needs to be a certain detachment from time, a certain monasticism in our lives.

In monasteries life is regulated by a bell. Monks and nuns know that time is not their own, that when the bell rings they must drop whatever they are doing and move on to what is being asked of them next. When the bell rings, St. Benedict said, the monk must put down his pen without crossing his "t" or dotting his "i." He must move on, not necessarily because he feels like doing something else, but because it is time—time to eat or pray or work or study or sleep. Monks' lives are regulated by a bell, not because they do not have watches and alarm clocks, but to remind them, always, that time is not their own and that there is a proper time to do things. Monks do not get to sleep, eat, pray, work, or relax when they feel like it, but when it is time to do those things.

There is an astonishing parallel between that and what happens in our own lives and we can be helped by understanding it. There is an in-built monasticism to our lives. We too, at least for the more active years, are called to practice a certain asceticism regarding time—to have our lives regulated by "the bell."

In our case "the bell" takes a different form, though its demands are the same as those of the bell in a monastery. In our case the bell is an alarm clock and the dictates of our daily lives: a quick breakfast, a commute to work (carrying sandwiches for lunch), staying home with small children, demands at work or at home, driving kids for lessons, dealing with them and their demands, household chores, cooking, laundry, taking out garbage, calling in a plumber, church on Sundays. Like monks we sleep, rise, eat, pray, and work, not necessarily when we would like to, but when it is time.

And this is true, not just for our daily routine, but as well for the seasons of our lives. We go to school, we prepare for a career, we enter the work force, are tied down with kids, mortgage payments, car payments, and the demands of family and work, not necessarily because we always feel like it, but because it is that time in our lives. The play of children and the leisure of retirement come before and after that season.

During all of the most active years of our lives we are reminded daily, sometimes hourly, that time is not our own; we are monks practicing a demanding asceticism.

There will not always be time to smell the flowers and we are not always poorer for the fact. Monasticism has its own spiritual payoffs. To be forced to work, to be tied down with duties, to have to get up early, to have little time to call your own, to be burdened with the responsibility of children and the demands of debts and mortgages, to go to bed exhausted after a working day is to be in touch with our humanity. It is too an opportunity to recognize that time is not our own and that any mature spirituality makes a distinction between the season for work and the sabbath, the sabbatical, the time of unpressured time.

Most important of all, recognizing in our duties and pressures the sound of the monastic bell actually helps us to smell the flowers, to give to each instant of our lives the time it deserves—and not necessarily the time I feel like giving it. We are better for the demands that the duties of state put on us, despite constant fatigue. Conversely, the privileged who have all the time in the world are worse off for that, despite their constant opportunity to smell the flowers. Monks have secrets worth knowing—and the pedagogy of a monastic bell is one of them.

Monasticism and the Playpen

There is a tradition, strong among spiritual writers, that we will not advance within the spiritual life unless we pray at least an hour a day privately.

I was stressing this one day in a talk, when a woman asked how this might apply to her, given that she was at home with young children who demanded her total attention.

"Where would I ever find an uninterrupted hour each day?" she moaned. "I would, I am afraid, be praying with children screaming and tugging at my legs."

A few years ago, I might have been tempted to point out to her that if her life was that hectic then she, of all people, needed time daily, away from her children, for private prayer among other things. As it was I gave her different advice:

"If you are at home alone with small children whose needs give you little uninterrupted time, then you don't need an hour of private prayer daily. Raising small children, if it is done with love and generosity, will do for you exactly what private prayer does."

Left unqualified, that is a dangerous statement. It suggests in fact that raising children is a functional substitute for prayer. However, in making the assertion that a certain service—in this case raising children—can in fact be prayer, I am bolstered by the testimony of contemplatives themselves.

Carlo Carretto, one of our century's best spiritual writers, spent many years in the Sahara Desert by himself, praying. Yet he once confessed that he felt that his mother, who spent nearly thirty years raising children, was much more contemplative than he was, and less selfish.

If that is true, and Carretto suggests that it is, the conclusion we should draw is not that there was anything wrong with his long hours of solitude in the desert, but that there was something very right about the years his mother lived an interrupted life amid the noise and demands of small children.

John of the Cross, in speaking about the very essence of the contemplative life, writes: "But they, O my God and my life, will see and experience your mild touch, who withdraw from the world and become mild, bringing the mild into harmony with the mild, thus enabling themselves to experience and enjoy you" (*The Living Flame of Love*, 1977).

In this statement John suggests there are two elements that are crucial to the contemplative's experience of God: withdrawal from the world and the bringing of oneself into harmony with the mild.

Although his writings were intended primarily for monks and contemplative nuns who physically withdraw from the world so as to seek a deeper empathy with it, his principles are just as true for those who cannot withdraw physically.

Certain vocations, for example, raising children, offer a perfect setting for living a contemplative life. They provide a desert for reflection, a real monastery.

The mother who stays at home with small children experiences a very real withdrawal from the world. Her existence is certainly monastic. Her tasks and preoccupations remove her from the centers of social life and from the centers of important power. She feels removed.

Moreover, her constant contact with young children, the mildest of the mild, gives her a privileged opportunity to be in harmony with the mild and learn empathy and unselfishness.

Perhaps more so even than the monk or the minister of the Gospel, she is forced, almost against her will, to mature. For years, while she is raising small children, her time is not her own, her needs have to be put into second place, and every time she turns round some hand is reaching out demanding something. Years of this will mature almost anyone.

It is because of this that she does not need, during this time, to pray for an hour a day. And it is precisely because of this that the rest of us who do not have constant contact with small children need to pray privately daily.

We, to a large extent, do not have to withdraw. We can often put our own needs first. We can claim some of our own time. We do not work with what is mild. Our worlds are professional, adult, cold, and untender. Outside of prayer we run a great risk of becoming selfish and bringing ourselves into harmony with what is untender.

Monks and contemplative nuns withdraw from the world to try to become less selfish, more tender, and more in harmony with the mild. To achieve this they pray for long hours in solitude.

Mothers with young children are offered the identical privilege: withdrawal, solitude, the mild. But they do not need the long hours of private prayer—the demands and mildness of the very young are a functional substitute.

Just Too Busy to Bow Down

Theologian Jan Walgrave commented that our present age constitutes a virtual conspiracy against the interior life. That is a
gentle way of saying that, within our culture, distraction is
normal, prayer and solitude are not. There is little that is contemplative within our culture and within our lives.

Why is this? We are not, by choice or ideology, a culture set
against solitude, interiority, and prayer. Nor are we, in my
opinion, more malicious, pagan, or afraid of interiority than
past ages. Where we differ from the past is not so much in bad-
ness as in busyness, in hurriedness. We do not think contem-
platively because we never quite get around to it.

Perhaps the most apt metaphor to describe our hurried and
distracted lives is that of a car wash. When you pull up to a car
wash, you are instructed to leave your motor running, to take
your hands off the steering wheel, and to keep your foot off the
brake. The idea is that the machine itself will suck you through.

For most of us, that is just what our typical day does to us, it
sucks us through. We now have radios with alarm clocks,
which go off before the alarm actually wakes us. Hence we are
already stimulated before we are fully awake.

Then we rise to shower and dress and ready ourselves for
work, stimulated by news, music, commentary. Breakfast and
the drive to work follow the same pattern. We listen to the radio, engage in conversation, plan our agenda, stimulated and
preoccupied. We spend our day working, necessarily preoccupied, our minds on what we are doing. When we return home,
there is TV, conversation, activities, and preoccupations of all
kinds. Eventually we go to bed, where perhaps we read or
watch a bit more TV. Finally we fall asleep.

When, in all of this, did we take time to think, to be contemplative, to pray, to wonder, to appreciate, simply to enjoy, to be restful, to be grateful just for being alive, to be grateful for love, for health, for God? The day just sucked us through.

I suspect that your coffee circles are similar to mine. Where I live, in the few contemplative moments that we take, we sit around talking: "It's a rat race. We should do something. We drive too hurriedly, we live too impatiently, we eat too fast, we work too hard, we are too preoccupied, too busy, we don't take time to smell the flowers!" But nothing changes.

As Mark Twain said: "It's like the weather—everyone complains about it, but nobody does anything about it."

Socrates commented, "The unexamined life is not worth living." I suspect that our age would counter, "The unlived life is also not worth examining." We have taken to examining our lives less and less.

The effect of this is the same everywhere. We see it in the way we eat, in the way we drive, in our inability to relax, in our lack of humor and reflectiveness and—need I say—in our lack of prayer.

I do not want to be judgmental but I suspect that most persons in our culture pray very little, at least in terms of private prayer. I suspect that the average person's prayer life consists of a short hurried prayer in the morning, an even more distracted and hurried prayer before meals, and another hurried prayer before retiring at night. That's precious little.

But our inability to be contemplative does not only show itself in our lack of private prayer. That is merely a symptom of something more deeply amiss. What our hurried lifestyle and our propensity for distraction is really doing is robbing us of solitude. As solitude diminishes, life seems less and less worth living.

Ironically most of us crave solitude. As our lives grow more pressured, as we grow more tired, and as we begin to talk more about burnout, we fantasize about solitude. We imagine it as a peaceful, quiet place, ourselves walking by a lake, watching a peaceful sunset, sitting in a rocker by the fireplace. But even there we make solitude yet another activity, something we do. We attempt to take solitude like taking a shower. It is understood as something we stand under, endure, get washed by—and then return to normal life.

Solitude, however, is a form of awareness. It is a way of being present and perceptive within all of life. It is having a dimension of reflectiveness in our ordinary lives that brings with it a sense of gratitude, appreciation, peacefulness, enjoyment, and prayer. It is the sense, within ordinary life, that ordinary life is precious, sacred, and enough.

How do we develop such a dimension within our lives? How do we foster solitude? How do we get a handle on life so that it does not just suck us through? How do we begin to lay a foundation for prayer in our lives? How do we come to gratitude and appreciation within ordinary life?

Eric Fromm was asked to give a simple recipe for psychic health in a culture that is as pressured as ours. "A half-hour of silence once a day, twice a day if you can afford the time. That will do marvels for your health," he answered.

Fromm's answer was not intended to be a religious one. He was no Thomas Merton. But it might have come from Merton. I can think of no better spiritual advice to give to a culture that conspires against interiority.

Try prayer and silence. One half-hour a day. Twice a day, if you can afford the time. It will do marvels for your health. As well, in a culture that conspires against the interior life, it will be a political act.

Praying Through a Crisis

We all have our moments of chaos and crisis. Loss, death, sickness, disappointment, hurt, loneliness, hatred, jealousy, obsession, fear; these come into our lives and often we find ourselves overwhelmed by the darkness they cause.

What can we do about them? How can we pull ourselves out of the dark chaos they put us into?

The simple answer of course is prayer. But that answer is given far too simplistically. We have all heard the phrases, so true in themselves: "Pray it through! Take your troubles to the chapel! Give it to God! God will help you!"

I can speak only for myself, though I suspect that my experience has its parallels in other lives, and I have found that often when I try to pray through some deep hurt I find no relief and, at times, end up more depressed, more immersed in the chaos, and more obsessively self-preoccupied than before praying.

Often I end up sucking the prayer into my own narcissism.

Too often when we try to pray when hurting, the prayer serves not to uproot the hurt and the narcissism, but to root it even more deeply in self-pity, self-preoccupation, and darkness. We end up further letting go of God's Spirit and, instead, giving in to panic, fear, chaos, non-forgiveness, obsession, and resentment. In a word, to the posture of masturbation, of non-prayer.

Why? Is God not willing to help? Is it simply a question of patience? God will eventually help, but not yet?

God is always willing to help, and, yes, we must be patient; healing takes time. But there is more involved. When we pray and our prayers do not help, then we are praying incorrectly. I have learned this painfully through years of mistakes.

Prayer is a focus upon God, not upon ourselves. When we are hurting or obsessed, the problem is that we are able to think about only one thing, the object of our hurt or loss. That concentration becomes depressive, oppressively focusing us so much upon one thing that we are not free emotionally to think about or enjoy other things. Depression is an over-concentration.

For this reason, whenever we are caught up in depression, it is important that our prayer be completely focused upon God and not upon ourselves.

If we do what comes naturally when trying to "pray through a crisis," we will end up thinking about the crisis, wallowing in our own sufferings.

Instead of freeing ourselves from the sense of loss or obsession, we will pull the wound inwards, make the pain worse, and the depression even more paralyzing.

When we pray in a crisis we must force ourselves to focus upon God or Jesus or upon some aspect of their sacred mystery, and we must resist entirely the urge to relate that encounter immediately to our wounded experience.

Let me illustrate this with an example. Imagine yourself suffering the loss of someone you deeply loved. Hurt, unable to think about anything else, you go to pray. Immediately the temptation will be to focus upon your heart, your obsession. You will try to "talk it through," however sincerely. But the result will be disastrous. You will find yourself becoming more fixed upon what you are trying to free yourself from. Your depression will intensify.

Conversely, if you force yourself, and this will be extremely difficult, to focus upon God—for example, as God is revealed in some mystery of Christ's life—your depression will be broken. You will experience God, slowly but gently, widening again the scope of your heart and mind. With that will come an emotional loosening and freeing.

When a wounded child climbs into her mother's lap, she draws so much strength from the mother's presence that her wound becomes insignificant. So too with us when we climb into the lap of our great Mother God. Our crisis soon domesticates and comes into a peaceful perspective, not because it goes away, but because the presence of God so overshadows us.

But this means we must genuinely climb into the lap of God. Like the wounded child we must be focused upon the mother, not upon ourselves. Concretely this means that when praying in a crisis we must refuse to think about ourselves at all; we must refuse even to relate the mystery we are meditating to ourselves and our wound. Like a child, we must simply be content to sit and be held by the mother.

That will be hard, very hard, to do. Initially every emotion in us will demand that we focus ourselves back upon our hurt. But that is the key; do not do it!

Do not, under the guise of prayer, wallow further in hurt. Rather focus upon God. Then, like a sobbing child at her mother's breast, in silence we will drink that which nurtures and brings peace.

At the breast of God we drink the Holy Spirit, the milk of charity, joy, peace, patience, goodness, mildness, long-suffering, faith, chastity, hope, and fidelity. In that nourishment lies peace.

Getting Angry With God

A woman suffering from a curious resentment came to see me. She was angry at God. Her feelings were vague and not clearly focused, but she felt that somehow God was to blame for her unhappiness.

Life, she felt, was rapidly passing her by and she had already missed out on many chances for really living it. She was, and had been, a good woman, religious, moral, generous, living for others, faithful to her commitments.

Now in her mid-fifties she felt anger and resentment growing within her, an anger and resentment she was unable really to explain, accept, or control. She was confused and unhappy. On the one hand she did not regret her past life. She had been faithful, unselfish, and religious. Yet, on the other, with her youth, health, sexual prowess, and opportunities fading, she felt frustrated, unneeded, unfulfilled, used, locked-in, and haunted by the thought that perhaps she had never made a decision for herself in her whole life.

Viewed one way, her virtue seemed like an accident, a conspiracy of circumstances. She wondered whether she had really chosen this or whether it had been forced upon her. Whenever she felt like that she was filled with regret and resentment. She regretted that she had always been so moral, religious, and proper. In these moments too she would have to admit to herself that she secretly envied the amoral, the unvirtuous, all those who never felt, as she did, the yoke of domestication that eventually comes with morality and religion.

At the root of all this was the feeling that she had been had, seduced by God. God was to blame. God, she assured me, had always been just real enough to hold her, but never real enough to fulfill her, at least not emotionally.

So she was angry, and angry with herself for being angry.

She was full of resentment and full of guilt for being resentful. Prayer was difficult for her because she could not admit to herself that she was angry at God and so whenever she tried to pray it seemed artificial and contrived. What does one say to a person like that? One begins by pointing out that her resentment and anger are already a high form of prayer, at least potentially so.

Too often we are under the impression that God does not want us to struggle, since, as we see it, God prefers sheep who docilely acquiesce (even as we swallow hard on the bitterness that so spontaneously arises in the emotional, psychological, and sexual mechanisms that were built into us).

But God wants to be wrestled with. As Rabbi Heschel points out, ever since the days when Abraham argued with God over the fate of Sodom and Gomorrah, and Jacob wrestled with the angel, those close to God have also occasionally engaged in similar arguments.

The refusal to accept the harshness of God's ways in the name of his love is an authentic form of prayer. Indeed the prophets and saints were not always in the habit of simply saying, "Thy will be done." They often fought, challenged, squirmed, and begged as a way of saying, "Thy will be changed!" I suspect that they did sometimes annul divine plans. God wants to be struggled with, especially if we have been living in God's house for a while.

Why? Why would God want this? How can wrestling be a form of prayer? Wrestling can be a form of prayer precisely because it can be a form of love. People who live together in love for a long time must resolve many tensions. There is constant wrestling, much anger, and occasional bitterness. But the struggling together, if persevered in, always leads to a new depth in love.

The woman I am describing was in fact standing at the very edges of a new phase of love. She needed to pray through her bitterness first. As she stood at the edges of that new phase, bent under the weight of God's yoke, bitter and with the jealousy of Cain in her eyes, the same Father who had pleaded with the older brother of the prodigal son was also pleading with her, to enter a new circle, the circle of those who feel compassion for God.

Rabbi Heschel tells the story of a Polish Jew who became bitter and stopped praying "because of what happened in Auschwitz." Later, however, he began praying again. When asked why, he replied, "I felt sorry for God."

This man had reached a new phase of love, that of affinity, of compassion. God's concerns, God's cause, God's house were now his too. But such a point is only reached after struggle, when anger and bitterness are transformed.

God invites, and I dare say, enjoys the struggle. As Nikos Kazantzakis puts it:

Every person partakes of the divine nature in both spirit and flesh. The struggle between God and the human person breaks out in everyone, together with the longing for reconciliation. Most often this struggle is unconscious and short-lived. A weak soul does not have the endurance to resist the flesh for long. It grows heavy, becomes flesh itself, and the contest ends. The stronger the soul and the flesh, the more fruitful the struggle, and the richer the final harmony. God does not love weak souls and flabby flesh. The Spirit wants to have to wrestle with flesh that is strong and full of resistance.

May we all win—by losing!

6

A Heart With Many Rooms: Social Justice

When we come to the end of our pilgrimage and reach heaven, God will ask, "Where are the others?"

Charles Peguy

The Bosom of God Is Not a Ghetto

Our age is witnessing an erosion of Catholicism. The consequence of this, besides our drab somberness, is a polarization which, both in the world and in the church, is rendering us incapable of working together against the problems that threaten us all. Let me explain.

We are, I submit, becoming ever less catholic. What is implied here? What is slipping? What does it mean to be catholic?

The opposite of catholic is not Protestant. All Christians, Protestants or Roman Catholics, characterize their faith as catholic—as well as one, holy, and apostolic.

The word "catholic" means universal, wide. It speaks of a comprehensive embrace. It's opposite, therefore, is narrowness, pettiness, lack of openness, sectarianism, provincialism, factionalism, fundamentalism, and ideology.

To my mind, the best definition of catholic comes from Jesus himself, who tells us: "In my Father's house there are many rooms" (John 14:2).

In speaking of the Father's house, Jesus is not pointing to a mansion in the sky, but to God's heart. God's heart has many rooms. It can embrace everything. It is wide, unpetty, open, and antithetical to all that is factional, fundamentalistic, and ideological. It is a heart that does not divide things up according to ours and theirs.

Nikos Kazantzakis wrote: "The bosom of God is not a ghetto." That is another way of saying that God has a catholic heart. To affirm this, however, is not to say that, since God is open to all and embraces all, nothing makes any difference, we may do as we like, all morality is relative, all beliefs are equal, and nobody may lay claim to truth.

There is a false concept of openness that affirms that to embrace all means to render all equal. Jesus belies this. He affirms the universal embrace of God's heart without affirming, as a consequence, that everything is OK. His Father loves everyone, even as he discriminates between right and wrong.

Catholicism can be spoken of as slipping, in that, unlike God's heart, more and more it seems that our hearts have just one room. Today we are seeing a creeping narrowness and intolerance. Fundamentalism, with its many types of ideology, has infected us. This is as true in the secular world as in the church. Fundamentalism and the narrowness and consequent polarization it spawns are everywhere. But this needs to be understood.

We tend to think of fundamentalism as a conservative view that takes Scripture so literally as to be unable to relate to the world in a realistic way. But that is just one, and a very small, kind of fundamentalism. We see fundamentalism wherever we see a heart with just one room.

The characteristic of all fundamentalism is that, precisely, it seizes on to some fundamental value, for example, the wisdom of the past, the divine inspiration of Scripture, or the importance of justice and equality, and makes that the sole criterion for judging goodness and authenticity.

In that sense, the fundamentalist's heart has just one room: a conservative, liberal, biblical, charismatic, feminist, anti-feminist, social justice, anti-abortion, or pro-choice room. It judges you as good, acceptable, decent, sincere, Christian, loving, and worth listening to only if you are in that room. If you are not ideologically committed to that fundamental, complete with all the prescribed rhetoric and accepted indignations, then you are judged as insincere or ignorant, and in need of either conversion or of having your consciousness raised.

In the end, all fundamentalism is ideology and all ideology

is fundamentalism—and both are a heart with one room, a bosom that is a ghetto. That is the real un-catholicism.

Tragically too, at the heart of all fundamentalism and ideology, there is an absence of a healthy self-love and a healthy self-criticism. That is why fundamentalists and ideologues are all so defensive, hypersensitive, and humorless. It is because of this that the world and the church are so full of intolerance, anger, lack of openness, self-righteous condemnation, scapegoating, and academic and moral intimidation. There are too few rooms in our hearts!

Given this, it is not surprising that very little genuine dialogue ever takes place. Most attempts at it are little more than name-calling and cheerleading. Given this too, it is not surprising that the working out of personal neuroses is frequently confused with genuine commitment to causes.

In God's house there are many rooms. There is an embrace for everyone; rich and poor, conservative and liberal, irrespective of whether one is wearing silks or denims. God's house is a catholic house.

And "we must be catholic as our heavenly Father is catholic." We must create more catholic hearts and more catholic houses. And this is not a call to be wishy-washy relativists who affirm that everything is OK as long as you do it sincerely. Like Christ, we must discriminate between right and wrong and believe in a divine truth which judges the world.

But we must free ourselves from un-catholicism, from fundamentalism and ideology that create a heart with just one room.

Closed to Love, Open to Hate

We live in a time of pain and division. Daily, in the world and in the church, hatred, anger, and bitterness are growing. It is ever harder to live at peace with each other, to be calm, not to alienate someone just by being. There is so much wound and division around. Women's issues, poverty and social justice, abortion, sexual morality, questions of leadership and authority, issues of war and peace, and styles of living and ministry are touching deep wounds and setting people bitterly against each other. This is not even to mention issues such as personality conflicts, jealousy, greed, and sin, which habitually divide.

Our psychic temperature is on the rise and with it, as Jesus predicted, son is turning against father, daughter against mother, sister against brother. We are being divided.

It is no longer possible to escape taking a stand on these issues, and to take a stand on them is to make enemies, to have someone hate you, to be accused of being narrow, and to be alienated from other sincere persons. For anyone who is sensitive, this is the deepest pain of all.

Moreover, none of us ever approaches these issues in complete fairness and objectivity. We are wounded, whether we admit it or not. Knowingly and unknowingly, in all these issues we have been either oppressor or oppressed, and consequently we approach them either too full of wound or too defensive to see straight. In either case the temptation is to become bitter and to give in to the propensity to feel that we have the right to be angry, to hate certain people, to be self-righteous, and to dissociate sympathy and understanding from certain others. That is a tragic mistake.

Valid, painful, and imperative as these issues may be, reason, love, understanding, and long-suffering may never give

way to a progressive and militant bitterness that can irrevocably alienate. That is the road to hell because bitterness is hell.

Yet that is what is happening today. We are too easily giving in to the temptation to think that because we have been
wounded, or because others are wounded, we have the right
to hate, to withdraw our empathy, to think in terms of black
and white, and to be bitter.

It is getting worse. Bitterness, like cancer, is slowly infecting
more and more of Christ's body.

We need to read this, the sign of the times, and respond to it
out of the gospel. It is my submission that, given this bitterness,
the Christian vocation today, for a time, will be that of letting
ourselves bleed, in tears and tension, to wash out these wounds.

Let me illustrate what this means. Just to be alive in the
church today is to be caught in a painful tension. For example,
the issues of women's rights and social justice are, without
doubt, two of the primary challenges that the Holy Spirit is
giving our age. Yet Rome refuses to raise seriously the question of the ordination of women and it silences Leonardo Boff,
a voice for the poor. With that comes a wave of resentment,
bitterness, and hatred.

Daily I move in circles where people are bitter about these
issues and I find myself increasingly reluctant to defend
Rome's stance on them. On these two issues we are sitting on a
powder keg and a deadly bitterness is flowing from them.

Yet no serious Catholic can be cavalier about the church as
institution. As universal. Some 800 million Catholics cannot
travel together without compromise, frustration, impatience,
tears, rules, and traditions which at times might seemingly
strangle some of the life that the Holy Spirit is spawning.
When a universal church moves forward, it can only be in
baby steps.

So what does the Christian who wants to be faithful today do? Ignore Rome? Consider the women's movement and social justice as fads? Grow cynical? Mind his or her own business and let be what is? Say "the hell with them all"?

Since nothing else is possible for now, save bitterness, which must be rejected, the answer lies in a fidelity that accepts suffering. To be faithful today means to live in pain, in tension, in frustration, in seeming compromise, often hated by both sides.

Our call today is to reconcile by feeling the pain of all sides and by letting our pain and helplessness be a buffer that heals, the blood that helps wash the wound. As a simple start we can test how open-minded we are on all these issues by seeing how much pain we are in. Not to be in pain is not to be open-minded.

It is a time of pain for the church, a time when we will all feel some hatred, a time when above all we must keep our peace of mind, our inner calm of spirit, and our outer charity.

Most of all, it is time to resist bitterness and that hardness of spirit that dampens the Holy Spirit.

Social Justice and Contemplation

Some years ago Ernst Kasemann, the Scripture scholar, commented that the problem with the church is that, chronically, the liberals aren't pious and the pious aren't liberal. If only, he speculated, Christians could be both.

Today, I submit, this dichotomy exists in the church between social justice and contemplation. Invariably those most actively involved in social justice are not as deeply involved in contemplation. Conversely those on the front lines of contemplation are often glaringly absent in the arena of social justice.

This situation, while far from ideal, would be more acceptable, given different charisms and calls, a division of labor, and the fact that nobody can be on the front lines of everything, except for the fact that, most often, there is suspicion and mistrust between those who identify closely with one or the other of these.

Far from seeing each other as sister and brother in a common struggle, as persons with different charisms called to unblock different arteries within the body of Christ, more often than not these two spend more time fighting with each other than challenging a world that tends to ignore both of them.

There are salient exceptions of course, as will be mentioned later, but all too common is the case where social justice activists cynically accuse their less socially active brothers and sisters of excessively privatizing the Gospel; of confusing love with sentiment, with being nice; of neglecting Jesus' non-negotiable demand that we side with the poor; and of identifying Christian practice simply with church-going, with private prayer and private morality, especially sexual morality.

Why, this group asks, are those not actively involved with social justice forever talking about sexual morality and *Hu-*

manae Vitae, and never about the social encyclicals? Why are people so fanatical about abortion and then so calloused regarding poverty, women's rights, immigration, and capital punishment?

Those less active in social justice return the accusations. All too common is the angry and judgmental accusation that those most active in social justice no longer pray; that they have the gospel confused with Greenpeace; that they neglect the fact that Jesus' non-negotiable demands radically invade one's private world and are equally as demanding there, in the order of sexual morality and private charity, as they are in the area of social justice, and that talk of justice and equality for all is hopelessly compromised when it issues from hearts hardened to the unborn.

I think Kasemann's words are true here. The liberals are not pious and the pious are not liberal.

This is a bad situation. If we are to offer any kind of help to a world interested neither in social justice nor in contemplation, a world which, effectively, has written us off, then we had best become liberal and pious, contemplative and socially active, both at once.

In my opinion there is nothing more urgent on the Christian agenda than this question, the marriage between social justice and contemplation. Both sides on this issue have correctly sensed that survival is at stake.

Unless the issues surrounding justice, poverty, war, the ecology, ethnic rights, and women's rights are addressed we won't have a world in which to practice our piety. Conversely if private prayer, private morality, and contemplation die, then we will still somehow lose the world or, certainly, we will lose any world worth living in.

The signs of the times need to be read: Vatican II, the recovery of the social gospel, the growing affluence of First World Christians, the breakdown of marriage and family life, the ecological crisis, the rise of feminism, the threat of nuclear war, oppressive injustice in the Third World, and the shrinking size of our planet have conspired to make it vital, a matter of life and death, that we make a marriage between social justice and contemplation. If we do not, we have no future.

As mentioned earlier, some are already modestly etching out a path toward this: Dorothy Day and the Catholic Worker Movement, Catherine Doherty and the Madonna House apostolate, Richard Rohr and the Center for Action and Contemplation, Jim Wallis and Sojourners, Jean Vanier and Henri Nouwen and L'Arche, Sheila Cassidy and the Hospice movement, Gustavo Gutierrez with his brand of Liberation Theology which always puts justice, love, and grace together in the same breath, Mother Teresa with her directness in dealing with both God and the poor, Thomas Merton and Daniel Berrigan with their reflective approach to civil disobedience, and, of course, John Paul II and many bishops' conferences with their social encyclicals and pastoral letters on justice.

In these we see the beginnings of a path, some charting of the uncharted. Action and contemplation, private morality and social awareness, prophetic anger and understanding, liberalness and piety are being married. From their lead we should take our cue.

Make Your Welcome Hearty

In October 1933 Peter Maurin wrote the following poem and commentary in the *Catholic Worker*:

People who are in need
   and are not afraid to beg
give to people not in need
   the occasion to do good
for goodness sake.
Modern society calls the beggar
   bum and panhandler
   and gives him the bum's rush.
But the Greeks used to say
   that people in need
   are ambassadors of the gods.
Although you may be called
   bums and panhandlers
   you are in fact the ambassadors of God.
As God's ambassadors
   you should be given
   food, clothing and shelter
by those who are able to give it.
Mohammedan teachers tell us
   that God commands hospitality
and hospitality is still practiced
   in Mohammedan countries.
But the duty of hospitality
   is neither taught nor practiced
   in Christian countries.
The poor are no longer
   fed, clothed and sheltered

at personal sacrifice
but at the expense of the taxpayers.
And because the poor
  are no longer
  fed, clothed and sheltered
  at personal sacrifice
the pagans say about Christians,
  "See how they pass the buck."

Maurin goes on to comment that a church council of the fifth century obliged bishops to establish houses of hospitality in connection with every parish. These houses were open to the poor, the sick, the orphaned, the aged, and the needy of every kind. The idea was that one must always be ready to recognize Christ in the unfamiliar face, and so every parish and every home was to have its "Christ room" set aside to receive the ambassadors of God who appear in the form of the needy and the visiting.

Hebrews 13:2 asks us not to neglect hospitality, remarking that, in receiving strangers "some have entertained angels without knowing it."

Lately we have neglected hospitality. There has been a bad slippage. No longer in our parishes, homes, and hearts is there a "Christ room." Not only do we no longer see hospitality as a privilege, we no longer see it even as a duty. Maurin is right, the Islamic world is doing much better at it than we are.

Why is this so? Are we more selfish? Are we busier? Is Christianity as a religion less hospitable than Islam?

There are a number of reasons for the demise of our sense of hospitality. One of them, surely, is the one Maurin points out, we have turned the duty of hospitality over to government agencies, the taxpayer, social security, social services. They are asked to take care of the widow, the orphan, the aged, and the stranger. More important, though, the demise of hospitality has occurred because we have developed a sense of privacy and efficiency that militate against it.

Our culture is becoming ever more narcissistic and idiosyncratic, that is, more and more we have the attitude that things are our own. We speak of my space, my time, my family, my home, my community, my room, my stereo, my plans, my agenda, my friendships, my effectiveness, and even, in a way, of my church.

In such a context we allow other persons into our lives, our homes, our communities, and our churches most selectively. We are hospitable to our own, to those who meet our standards and our timetables. This invariably excludes the poor from our hearts, homes, and churches, since they have no sense of our standards and timetables. Their problems are neither antiseptic nor conveniently scheduled.

Compounding this is the problem of efficiency. When Thomas Merton was asked what he thought the worst problem was facing Western civilization, instead of answering with something like "injustice," "moral decay," or "lack of interiority," he replied simply, "Efficiency!"

Our problem in the Western world, everywhere from the Pentagon to our monasteries, is that the plant must run! The classes must be taught, the crops must be sown and harvested, the kids need to be driven for their lessons, the meeting must run as scheduled, the supper must be cooked, the essay needs to be written, the mortgage needs to be paid, the plane needs to be caught, things must keep running, there is no other way, the show must go on, we need to do what we need to do!

In all that, partly, we are losing our souls because in it there is no space or time for hospitality, and hospitality is the mark of a truly gracious soul.

Would that the hallmark of our Christian homes and churches be the graciousness of our welcome, and would that, when we die, each of us might be most remembered for our hospitality, the graciousness of our welcome!

It's Easy to Sacrifice Others

"It is better that one man should die for the people."

Why does that line have so haunting a sound? Why does it sound like the refrain of a litany? It haunts, not because of any particular poetic merit, but because it expresses a perverse truth that invariably fascinates. In a caption it rationalizes death, deals death, and justifies it.

Caiaphas, the high priest, first used this phrase to justify Christ's death. Christ's person and message were upsetting things, upsetting the way life had been, upsetting a delicate balance of relationships that had built up, like a complex ecology, over many years.

Caiaphas and the other leaders at that time did not in fact have a lot of personal things against Christ. They were just scared. There was more fear than malevolence present when Christ was condemned. It was fear that prompted Caiaphas to utter this phrase and so justify his acquiescence in an innocent death.

That fear, and that phrase, have always been the great rationalization for death and have justified our acquiescence in countless deaths; so much so that it is possible to construct a litany for death with this phrase as its refrain:

• When we favor capital punishment and support the idea that some persons, irrespective of what kind of lives they are leading, should be put to death, we are saying: better that one person should die for the people.

• When there is abortion, when an unborn child's life is taken, our society is saying: better that one person should die for the people.

• When we refuse to care properly for the poor in our society, when we say we cannot afford welfare, medicare, day care, free education, and the support of mothers at home with small children, when we let the poor fall through the cracks rather than upset our standard of living, we are saying: better that one person should die for the people.

• When someone is slandered in conversation and we, because of fear, say nothing, we are saying: better that one person should die for the people.

• When our countries bomb their neighbors to insure their own security, when our countries use unjustifiable amounts of money, talent, and resources to build up weapons of defence, we are saying: better that one person should die for the people.

• When our countries do not take refugees because we fear that they will take some of our jobs and have an adverse effect on our standard of living, we are saying: better that one person should die for the people.

• When our countries refuse to admit that so much of the discontent and terrorism of our age is the natural byproduct of a way of life, a system, wherein the rich benefit from the poor, when we do nothing about this because it would mean some very upsetting changes, we are saying: better that one person should die for the people.

• When, because of the pressures of our lifestyles, we draw too excessively upon the world's resources, when, for the same reason, we cannot properly respect nature and by exorbitant consumption and its concomitant pollution we destroy the environment for future generations, we are saying: better that one person should die for the people.

• When a youth gang in Montreal brutally murders a homosexual man with AIDS on a subway, when, in the mid-1960s, thirty-eight people in New York City watch a woman being murdered in a public place and, because of fear, refuse to intervene, both the aggressors and the bystanders (for different reasons) are saying: better that one person should die for the people.

• When Martin Luther King, Malcolm X, Oscar Romero, Erzy Popieluszko, Stan Rather, Michael Rodrigo, and Anne Frank are killed, when the KKK murders three civil rights workers in Mississippi in the early 1960s, when oppressive regimes around the world intimidate people and make them disappear, someone is saying: better that one person should die for the people.

Death's great litany echoing through the centuries, from Caiaphas to us—better that one person should die for the people, better this death than that our lives should be so upset, better this than that we should have to change!

Cardinal Jaime Sin of the Philippines once commented upon the place of courage within the spectrum of virtue:

> Strength without compassion is violence
> Compassion without justice is sentiment
> Justice without love is Marxism
> And...love without justice is baloney!

We all need greater courage. We need to pray for that. We need to pray to be less intimidated by our own weaknesses and fears, to be more courageous in moving beyond the comforts of affluence, privilege, and good name, to be less timid, less small, less petty, and more willing to sacrifice and perhaps even to die rather than to acquiesce in the death of an innocent person by uttering, however unreflectively and unconsciously, the phrase: better that one person should die for the people.

Alive with Prophetic Pain

I had a lengthy talk with a friend of mine who is a Catholic feminist. Articulate and not afraid to express her anger, she talked openly about her pain. She is frustrated with inequality in the church, frustrated that she can never be ordained. The tears flowed freely; she wanted to leave the church she had grown up in, but something held her back.

A day later, quite by chance, I was conducting a marriage interview and the young woman about to be married spoke tearfully about the same pain. She too was considering leaving the church.

In telling their stories, both commented that what was really pushing them to leave the church was the pain they experienced while attending the Eucharist. Both were filled with pain, anger, and bitterness and were reduced to tears.

Superficially, one might conclude that their pain is most acute at Eucharist because a male presides there. But this, I submit, is a secondary explanation. Their pain touches on something deeper that must send a signal to the whole church. Irrespective of the fact that their pain is mixed with other pains, the women are experiencing the pain of the prophet.

Scripture states that prophets die somewhere between the altar and sanctuary. Given that, should it be so surprising that people will experience their deepest pains at liturgy? Given too that the church had best be looking at and listening to those who feel killed at the Eucharist, namely, those who have to die a little to stand in the sanctuary, we had best embrace those persons and this pain for the sake of the church and its health. And we had better tell those persons how important it is that they do not leave us.

Both women were convinced that this kind of pain at the

Eucharist indicates it is best they should leave. However, their pain is prophetic. It indicates that something is amiss, but amiss with the whole body, not with one individual. Their pain also indicates that the Eucharist in fact is effective. By its very nature it is meant to be a place of anguish as well as a place of celebration. The Eucharist is meant to break us open, to break us down, to grind and transubstantiate us into one community of love.

Since we come to the Eucharist far from united, each of us trapped in his or her own narcissism and selfishness, we need to be broken down before unity and community can take place. This does not happen without pain and anguish. But it is not necessarily those who feel the most anguish who most need to be broken down or changed. Their pain indicates that there is something wrong in the body.

I am heartened in the faith, even if not delighted emotionally, when I hear of someone who fills with anguish at the Eucharist. It means that she or he is sincere, that she or he has deep roots within the Eucharistic community, and that the Eucharist is still working.

And these, the ones who fill with pain, need to be specially embraced and listened to. Those who feel oppressed, excluded, and who die (in whatever way) in the sanctuary are most often the prophetic voices, even if they themselves are inarticulate. Their pain is not.

Karl Barth stated that in the incarnation God descends, moving from "height to the depth, from victory to defeat, from riches to poverty, from triumph to suffering, from life to death." In those who suffer, God is revealed—and this is nowhere more true than at the Eucharist.

"Pain" is a word. Like God's spirit it gives expression to what is too deep for words. Pain, accepted without final bitter-

ness and persevered in, is prophecy. It is God's voice in a calloused church and world. It comes from conscience and speaks
to conscience.

In the Eucharist, among other things, the passion and death
of Christ are being re-enacted. Obviously those who are suffering the most and are doing some dying are the Christ figures.

That is why it is so important that those who feel like these
women, those who fill with pain and tears at the Eucharist, remain in the church and remain at the Eucharist. Without prophetic tears, we grow ever more deaf. And prophets die somewhere between altar and sanctuary. But their groan is a word,
a voice, that cannot be killed.

7

Signs of the Times: Keeping One's Balance in a Complex World

There is no short-cut, no easy road, to wisdom. After all the centuries of invention, the soul's path lies through the thorny wilderness which must be still trodden in solitude, with bleeding feet, with sobs for help, as it was trodden by them of old time.

George Eliot

Keeping Your Faith in Balance

I share with you here four tales of imbalance. Each is the story of a person who is sincere, Christian, and dedicated, but has fallen from wholeness. From these stories of imbalance, I hope, we will be able to see where proportion lies.

A tale of the neglect of social justice
A bishop I know recounts this story. One day he received a phone call from an angry woman.

"Why, " she demanded, "are you and the other bishops so hung up on social justice? Why don't you stick with what the church is all about: liturgy, prayer, and morality?"

He answered her with another question, "What would you do if you were a bishop and someone called you and said: 'Our parish priest refuses to preach about private prayer and private morality. He tells us that these are fads that a few contemplatives have started. They are not important in the Christian life'?"

"I would suspend the man on the spot!" was her reply.

"Then," replied the bishop, "what am I to do with a person who phones and says: 'Our priest refuses to preach social justice. He tells us that this is just a fad started by the liberation theologians and a few social-justice types. You can be a good Christian and never practice social justice'?"

This woman's question betrays a dangerous imbalance. Spirituality is reduced to prayer and private morality. As important as these are, they are not enough.

A tale of the neglect of prayer and private morality
Some years ago while doing graduate work, I was working as a chaplain at a hostel in a poorer section of San Francisco. One of the persons I was working with, a very dedicated person, said to me:

"Father, do you really think God gives a damn whether you say your morning and evening prayers, whether you hold a grudge, or whether you hop in and out of bed a few times with someone you aren't married to? These small, private things are so unimportant.

"What possible difference do they make in the light of the larger questions of peace and justice? God hasn't got time for our private little prayers and little moral struggles!"

For him spirituality meant the struggle for peace and justice, the taking care of God's poor. Just that. Private prayer and private morality were so dwarfed by these larger issues as to seem unimportant.

As important as is the struggle for peace and justice, being a prophet implies more.

A tale of the neglect of joy and celebration

I attended an international conference in Belgium on local church that brought together people from all parts of the world. On the second-to-last day the organizers called a halt to work, to all the discussing and theologizing. We were all sent off to the beautiful city of Bruges for tours, cocktails, dining, and celebrating.

In my own group was a young nun from the Third World. There was no doubt that she was a woman who prayed, whose private morals were beyond suspicion, and that her whole life was being lived for the poor. But she struggled, and deeply, to be joyful, to celebrate, and not to be angry and bitter. She found our half-day celebration a tough chore, an evil to be endured, a waste of time, and an insult to the poor. Again, I submit, there is here an imbalance. What is lacking in this woman's life? Certainly not prayer, private morality, or a preferential option for the poor.

What is lacking is friendship, celebration, and the greatest asceticism of all, that of being a joyful, celebrating, and non-bitter person. Prophetic witness lies as much in being a happy and non-bitter person as in being a person of prayer, morality, and social justice, though admittedly the former is based a lot on the latter.

A tale of the neglect of love

After I delivered a talk on prophecy, a woman challenged me. "You spoke too little about anger! You were too soft. Prophecy is all about challenge, anger, and righteousness. Without a proper anger, you cannot be prophetic!"

She said more, mostly about the need for anger and a bitter challenge to the mainstream culture.

Again, at least in her challenge to me, there was imbalance. She spoke constantly of anger, of challenge, of criticalness. Never once did she mention love. Her attitude toward the culture was that of disdain, bitterness, anger, and disgust. Nowhere in her did I detect compassion, sadness, sympathy, or love toward or about those she was supposedly preaching to.

A prophet, as Jim Wallis suggests, is always characterized more by love than by anger. Likewise, as psychology points out, we can only truly challenge another to change if that other first feels loved by us.

There are certain non-negotiable prongs within Christian spirituality: prayer and private morality, a commitment to justice and peace, the discipline of joy and celebration (that is, the Christian duty to be a happy person), and the duty to challenge by love.

And the key to health is proportion.

Listening to Different Voices

I am particularly fond of biography. Stories of people's lives, save for the cheaper accounts of the lives of the rich and famous, are a special kind of literature. A good story throws light on everyone's life since, as Willa Cather says, "There are only two or three human stories, and they go on repeating themselves as fiercely as if they had never happened."

This is even more true when we are dealing with the story of someone of our own generation who, even though his or her life may be different from ours, has felt the changes of the world at the same time we did. There is a certain affinity, compassion, con-naturality, and even a mysticism among those who experience the same things at roughly the same time.

Where were you when Kennedy was shot? Do you remember the cold war, the fall-out shelters, the advent of Presley, the Beatles, hard rock, hard drugs, Woodstock, the Vietnam War, the world going crazy in 1968?

Do you remember the time before the sexual revolution, Vatican II, the slide of marriage and family life, the hopeless fragmentation of knowledge, and the anger, polarization, and yuppyism of the 1980s?

These events were the acid, we are the litmus paper. Most of us, I suspect, turned the same colors.

Given that affinity among us, I want to share part of my own story. Not because it is in any way extraordinary, but precisely because it is so ordinary and typical. I want to describe some of the colors I have turned and am still turning. Perhaps it will be helpful in dealing with your own story since we share a common place in history. We have been dropped in the same test tube.

I am a child of our age and, for this reason, straddle two cultures and am subject to two voices. The earliest voice that spoke to me was that of my parents and of their culture. They were immigrants, economically poor, pious, Christian. So was their culture.

Their voice spoke as follows. Worldly success is not important. What is important are Christ, family, church. Duty and self-sacrifice are more important than personal fulfillment. Life here in this world is not so important. We can live in dissatisfaction and frustration since, before death, we live as in a valley of tears, in a world in which the symphony can never be finished. Ecstasy must be postponed until the next life. Personal morality, especially if it has to do with sex, is a big deal. So too is private prayer. You should be charitable to the poor. (There was little talk of social justice since we were, in fact, the poor.) The world is a cold and pagan place, set over against the church. The voice said: Be suspicious, always suspicious, of the world and its ways.

But already as a child another voice and another culture began to seep in. I read magazines, listened to the radio, watched TV and movies, looked at catalogues and travel brochures, and began to read a literature that spoke in another voice. Each year too I watched events irrevocably changing our lives and our culture.

This new voice spoke as follows. You are poor now, but you can move from rags to riches. You were born the immigrant, but you can live as something else. Family, church, and Christ are important, but so too is success, a career. Make something of yourself. Be admired. Duty and sacrifice need sometimes to be jettisoned for personal fulfilment; after all, you only live once and there is meant to be some life after birth (as well as after death). Private prayer and private morality, including sexual ethics, are not such a big deal. Do not be suspicious of the world. It often affirms life where the church does not. Be suspicious instead of the church and its hang-ups, timidities, and fears. Look at where it blocks life.

I have spent most of my life caught between these two voices —confused, stretched, unsure, torn, testing one, then the other.

One of these voices, that of my parents, has won an essential victory. But that victory is still bitterly contested and is far from complete and unequivocal.

Parts of me belong to the culture that was not my parents', and these sometimes win their own kind of victory. Moreover, in head and heart it is not so clear that one voice, my parents', is everywhere identifiable with Christ's voice and that the other voice is always identifiable with the world.

My parents' culture had its faults. It could be racist, bigoted, prejudiced, narrow, timid, and unhealthily fearful. Invariably there was the timidity of the immigrant, the bias of the ghetto: "Us against them," "Stay with your own kind," "Don't even selectively try to love what's outside."

As well, the other voice, despite its obvious bias for the world, speaks of a universalism, an openness, and a challenge beyond fear and timidity that echoes the gospel better than the voice of my parents' culture.

So where does that leave me? Living a question. Uncertain of a lot of things. Steady in some convictions, gasping for oxygen in others. Convinced that old-time religion and fundamentalism are not the answer, but suspicious that perhaps I, we, somehow need to be inner immigrants.

Beyond those questions, though, is a growing comfort, totally undeserved, to be sure, in a surer knowledge that we are loved by God, myself no less than everyone else.

Given that comfort, I feel no panic about the two voices. Being pulled between them is quite an adventure.

Being Normal Is Not Our Goal

In an interview in the *National Catholic Reporter*, Richard McBrien suggests that the Roman Catholic church ought to change its law regarding priestly celibacy. His argument is as straightforward as it is convincing: "I mean, healthy people are sexually active people. That's normal. So why do we make priests behave as if they're not healthy and normal?" (January 20, 1989)

The functions and dysfunctions of priestly celibacy might be debated, as might McBrien's argument. What has implications in that statement for issues far beyond clerical celibacy is the appeal to normalcy as the criterion for health and rightness, "That's normal. So why are we acting otherwise?"

That is very persuasive and powerful. What is healthy is normal. To deviate from that imperative is to risk sickness. One must act as normal people do.

There is much truth in that. There are serious risks in thinking one can be healthy and yet live differently than normal persons.

The proof of the pudding is in the eating and, as McBrien goes on to point out, celibacy does in fact take its toll upon the lives of many priests who end up unhealthy—succumbing to alcohol, a rationalized double life, gadgetry, compensating consumption, or repressed sexuality that frequently then manifests itself in the abuse of power.

What is true here for celibacy is also true for many other areas wherein religion, or anything else, asks a person to live what most others are not living. For example, in monasticism (as well as more recently in social justice circles) one sees a dark side among some: weirdness, repression of need, elitist self-righteousness, neuroses, and anger paraded as sanctity, and, as in clerical celibacy gone sour, the misuse of power. One takes a very serious risk in not letting what is more normal adjudicate health.

However, with that being admitted, Goethe might aptly be quoted: "The risks of life are many, and safety lies among them." The gospel asks of us risk, to put out into the deep waters. This demand, if followed, will precisely displace us from what we would like to live as normal life. Let me explain.

The word church comes from the word *ecclesia*, from the Greek (*ek*–out of; *kaleo*–to call). To be a member of the church is to be called out of something.

What are we called out of? Precisely, normal life, as unchallenged human propensity would like to define it.

Outside of a challenge from something beyond us we automatically identify what is normal with what most people are living at a given time. Normalcy by popular consensus. Health and sanctity defined by Gallup poll.

When this happens then invariably normalcy identifies itself with idiosyncratic preference, the good life: a good job, a good romance, a good house, good vacations, good sex, a good body, and enough money, freedom, and leisure to enjoy it all. That is what all of us normal people in fact want.

Baptism into Christian life is meant to be a displacement from that. It is meant, precisely, to call us out of that normalcy. It is meant to derail us, to put a belt around us and lead us where we would rather not go.

Entry into church is, to use an older phrase, a consecration. That word too, like church, means displacement, derailment.

For most of us "consecration" is a pious, sacristy word. It speaks of consecrated chalices, altars, churches. Of itself, that is not an improper use of the word. To consecrate something is to displace it from normal use: an ordinary cup is set aside to become a chalice, an ordinary table is set aside to become an altar, or an ordinary building is set aside to become a church.

When we think of consecration in that sense however, it generally takes on such connotations of piety and separateness that it means little to us in ordinary life. Let me attempt another way of explaining this: To be consecrated is to be displaced from normalcy.

Imagine yourself setting out on vacation. You have planned your trip in detail and are eagerly looking forward to enjoying this well-deserved rest. You pack the car and go. On the way you come upon a serious traffic accident. Some people are hurt and dying. There is no one else around. At that moment you become consecrated. Your holiday plans must be, for the moment, set aside, displaced, with the rest of normal life. A very legitimate agenda must be set aside.

Christian life displaces in the same way. It sets aside what we would, without baptism, define as normal life.

A friend of mine who is deeply committed to family, church, and social issues is, when overwhelmed and frustrated, fond of saying, "If there is reincarnation in my next life, I am coming back as a yuppie. I'll have nothing to do with having kids, church, or the poor. I'll have season tickets to everything, go on a lot of ski trips, and let God take care of his own world."

There is as much wisdom as self-pity in that remark. It speaks of a genuine baptism, of a life that has been consecrated in that the needs of the kingdom have derailed plans for a more selfish fulfilment.

The human instinct is to define the normal by idiosyncratic preference and social consensus. We need to challenge this if religion is to have an agenda that includes celibacy, social justice, or anything else that goes against what most people are in fact living.

High Season for Religion Foes

These are tough days for those who believe in the institutional church and in organized religion. Daily our newspapers document incidents of sin, corruption, abused power, misguided fanaticism, and betrayed trust—all done in the name of religion or under its guise! Pedophilia among Roman Catholic priests, sex and money scandals among TV evangelists, hostage-taking and bombings by fundamentalist Arabs, Irish Catholics, and Hindu Sikhs—these and other lesser scandals fill the front pages. As one commentator put it, "This is the church's Watergate!"

Many people's faith is shaken; understandably so. Trust, once given then betrayed, is not easily restored. Faith in organized religion is difficult at the best of times and so, given all this disillusionment, it is becoming ever easier for people to believe that they would best go through life independent of the institutional church. Moreover, for those who despise or ignore organized religion (cultured agnostics, religious lone-rangers, anti-clericals), this is high season.

What all these scandals are doing is helping confirm their most hopeful suspicions. Religion is a hoax; organized church practice serves the interests of those who organize it; Roman Catholic celibacy is a front; everyone has an angle; in the church, as elsewhere, sex and money are what it's ultimately all about; the institutional part of religion is what corrupts faith; pure self-sacrifice does not exist within the churches; one is best off without organized religion; Jesus founded a kingdom, humans created the churches. All these Watergate-type revelations are finally revealing the truth! What is to be said and done in the face of all of this?

All healing begins with a lancing of the wound. We should,

despite the pain and humiliation of this, be grateful that the truth is being exposed. In the long run the truth will set us free.

In the short run the prognosis is less positive. We have to be prepared for a season, perhaps a very long one, of continued pain and embarrassment and a further erosion of trust. We have to accept this and accept it without self-pity, rationalization, half-baked justifications, or any attempts to water down the seriousness of what is revealed in these scandals. Partly we are sick and, like a virus that has infected the body, this has to run its course, and the body, in pain and fever, has to build up a new immune system. In the short run we can only do what Lamentations advises: "Put your mouth to the dust and wait!"

Beyond that, those of us who are not directly involved in these scandals, either personally or institutionally, must resist the temptation to distance ourselves and our churches from them with the attitude, "Don't look at me; I'm innocent. This is somebody else's problem!"

It is our problem, irrespective of whether we are innocent or guilty. All Christians, along with all other sincere believers, form one body. Christ's body. We are all in this together, with Christ. We may not facilely link ourselves with our church's graced moments, its saints, martyrs, and proud achievements, and then slickly distance ourselves from its dark history, its compromises, its perverseness, its pedophilia, and its sex and money scandals. To be a member of the church, to be a believer, is to be linked to all of this, grace and sin.

In this context is it significant to point out that Christ died between two thieves. He was innocent; they were not. However, because his sacrifice was seen against that horizon, it was judged by association, by those present, to be as tainted as the deaths of those he died with. People watching the crucifixion did not distinguish between who was guilty and who was in-

nocent. They assessed what they saw *en bloc*. For them all cru-
cifixions meant the same thing.

The church is still judged in the same way. To be a church
member is still to be connected, by association, with sin and
sinners. Christ was the object of suspicion and misunderstanding. Every kind of accusation was leveled against him. This
will be true, always, of his church.

Like him, the church will always be seen by outsiders as
framed against a certain horizon—on display with scoundrels,
child molesters, fakes, frauds, bad thieves, and good thieves.
The crucifixion of Christ is still going on and it is mixed in
with the personal tragedies of honest and dishonest sinners.
Christ is always pinned up among thieves.

But the church need offer no particular apologetics for this.
The historical Jesus was found there. Why should the church
not be found there?

As the great Protestant theologian Friedrich Schleiermacher
stated, already a century ago, in *Speeches to the Cultured Despis-
ers of Religion* (new edition 1958), the temptation is always to
despise religion in its positive form, that is, in its concrete historical expression in the churches where it finds itself hopelessly and inextricably intertwined with the sin, pettiness, and
foibles of ordinary human beings. Invariably the temptation is
to say, "I can handle God, but I won't be involved with all this
human mess we call the church!"

To speak that line is to utter the greatest ecclesial heresy
there is. To speak it is also to abandon the true Christ for an
idol. Jesus walked with sinners, ate with them, was accused
with them, and died with them. The church is true when it is
in solidarity with him, especially in that. Lately the church has
been dying a lot with sinners. It has been a humiliating experience—but then, so was the crucifixion!

Abortion: No Quick Solutions

For more and more of us, I suspect, the issue of abortion brings up feelings of helplessness that border on despair. The issue is so important that a conscientious person may not remain silent for long without incurring guilt.

But what responses are truly productive? What can genuinely help change this situation? What would Jesus do? Would he organize political lobbies? Lobby for pro-life candidates? Withhold portions of his income tax? Demonstrate outside abortion clinics? Chain himself to a fence?

I honestly do not know. There is in me neither the vision nor the will to try to answer those questions. What I do want to offer, and hesitantly at that, are the rather meager fruits from my own struggles with these questions. I have always been, and remain uncompromisingly pro-life. Rightly or wrongly, however, I have not always been involved in the active struggle, the political organizing, and the demonstrations. Why?

Sometimes I rationalize that if God had wanted me to be a prophet, he would have given me greater strength and a less ambiguous vision. As it is, I am Germanic, complete with the proclivity for procrastination and the need for the infallible assurance, before I act, that I am not making a mistake. But, these things aside, my hesitation has also been based upon a belief that this issue, for all its urgency, has no quick solution.

To begin to explain this, I need to speak about power. What kind of power may we seize upon to try to change this situation? Too many people, I am afraid, have placed their hopes in legal power, political power. The belief is that if we work hard enough we can get the laws changed, put abortionists on trial, close down abortion clinics. To this end we demonstrate, withhold taxes, organize lobbies, and chain ourselves to fences. I am not suggesting that these things do not need to be done; after all, real people are dying. This battle is more than academic.

And yet the only real solution is long-range. This battle, in the end, cannot be won legally and politically. Ultimately, more than laws, hearts need to be changed. Conversion is the only effective way of ultimately ending abortions. Abortion clinics will shut down when nobody shows up at their doors any more.

To win the battle politically, without a conversion of hearts, will simply roll back the clock, drive people into illegal backroom clinics, allow abortionists like Henry Morgenthaler to posture as martyrs, and lead to a renewed effort on the part of the pro-abortionists. It will be a temporary slowing down of abortions, at best.

Moreover, this conversion must involve a conversion within relationships. Today the issue of abortion cannot be fairly thought out because radical feminism has claimed pro-choice as one of its key liberation items. To be "pro-life" is to be classified as "anti-feminist."

This is tragic for both sides on this issue because, consequently, sincere men and women are forced to distance themselves from feminism; and feminists, on their part, are all too often forced to distance themselves from one of the things they would most need to change in order to bring about healthier relationships between women and men: the stopping of abortion.

Radical feminism has seen, and rightly so, a connection between the abortion issue and feminine oppression. Unfortunately it has not always, in my opinion, understood that connection correctly, even as it intuited its gravity. The oppression of women in our culture is especially sexual. In a sexually irresponsible culture the inevitable losers are women. They end up suffering the most.

When a culture exists in which men and women do not trust each other, in which sexual irresponsibility is encouraged in (and even, at times, forced upon) young people, and in which women— for reasons that are often far beyond their free choosing—sleep with and conceive children from men they hardly know, you inevitably have abortion.

But it is not the girl or woman who shows up at the abortion clinic who is most to blame, nor perhaps even the boy or man who impregnates her. We are all to blame. The lady who stands before the abortionists is, with her child, victim, the tip of a pine cone of irresponsibility and oppression. And on her part, abortion is an act of resignation. No woman ever really wants an abortion and no woman is ever happy for having had one. As Ginny Soley puts it:

> Abortion is, finally, an act of despair. The decision to have an abortion reflects a woman's lack of confidence in herself. It means that she does not trust the man with whom she is in relationship. It means that she has no belief in long-lasting, long-term, stable relationships between men and women. In fact it means that she has lost confidence in life itself. (*Sojourners*, October 1986)

The road to final victory on the issue of abortion is long, the task mammoth. Hearts need to change, relationships need to change, sexual patterns need to change, oppression needs to be recognized; and real villains and real victims must be more accurately named.

Pro-life and Anti-abortion

The next few years will be decisive regarding the question of abortion. The battle will be definitely lost or won.

We have had, in the Western world, abortion on demand for more than a decade. However, this has never sat easy. There has been, even as the movement plowed irresistibly and seemingly irrevocably forward, a massive growth of resistance. That resistance has ripened just at a time when governments, for a variety of reasons, are being forced to re-examine the laws that have given us abortion on demand.

During the next few years, certainly in North America, new laws will be brought in or old laws will be upheld that will, I fear, cement the issue into one mold or the other for a long time. Consequently, the time is critical for pro-life. People tend to accept as OK whatever they have gotten used to. Practice becomes custom, custom becomes law, legality is seen as morality. Our culture is used to abortion on demand. The longer this persists the more irrevocable it becomes.

Given this situation and the present political state, there is a chance, a last chance perhaps for a long time, to again instill in our political system the will to protect the unborn. But we must act quickly and massively.

Many of us are not used to acting regarding this question. We are pro-life, but in a rather antiseptic way. Pro-life is part of our curriculum vitae: we are officially pro-life; we offer it moral support; we write articles and make statements about its place within the wider spectrum of social justice; but we are entirely absent from the picket lines and from any direct lobbying or confrontational process.

I have been an antiseptic pro-lifer. I have written an article a year against abortion, spoken out against it in my classrooms, and even addressed pro-life groups, but I have not walked a picket line, written or phoned a member of the legislature, or realistically confronted anyone on this issue for fifteen years. Given this background, I was deeply cut, as one is when a truly prophetic word is heard, by an editorial, "An open letter to socially concerned Catholics: resist abortion now!" in *Catholic New Times*, June 25, 1988.

Since there are out there, I suspect, many other antiseptic pro-lifers like myself, I share with you by way of a brief precis some of the salient points of that very prophetic editorial.

One of the most unfortunate developments within the church and within society at large is the phenomenon wherein both conservative and liberal Christians tend to lack a consistent approach to pro-life.

Liberals, while clamoring loudly for social justice in the areas of economics, racial and sexual discrimination, immigration laws, housing, and Third World concerns, have been simply tolerant of and silent about abortion.

Conservatives, on the other hand, have championed the fight against abortion, but have frequently reduced the concern for life to a simple anti-abortion focus. Thus, while speaking clearly in favor of life on one front, they have been noisily in favor of capital punishment, nuclear arms, and the system of liberal capitalism (which sees society as a system of competing individual rights that must be legally bartered). As well, they have been less fully for life in their views regarding women.

However, with that said, the editorial goes on to praise the conservatives' pro-life efforts. Pro-life groups, despite being single-issue focused and inconsistent in the support of life, have nonetheless "borne the political heat of the day on the issues of abortion. And they have borne it with courage." Their passion is a welcome challenge.

Tolerant liberals, who often find pro-life tactics distasteful, would do well to examine themselves and see whether they are backing off from the abortion issue because of the current sense of what is socially acceptable.

The editorial goes on to say that the social virtues of tolerance may never be invoked "to legitimate the decertifications of the unborn as human beings." The work of justice, it asserts, is "totally lacking in integrity if, by omission or commission, we participate in the bartering away of the rights of the smallest and weakest members of our society."

Moreover, we may not believe "that the rights of a woman, or of any other group, will be served as long as the rights of one group, the unborn, can be negotiated out of existence. A society which assumes the divine right of deciding when life begins will all too easily move on to decide when it should end and for whom."

Such a clear stand on abortion does not, the article rightly asserts, diminish the sincerity and admirable social commitment of many pro-choice persons. Nor does it withhold compassion for or judge those who have had abortions. It simply offers a consistent ethic for life and, prophetically, stands up for those who have the least voice. Finally and importantly, it calls upon all of us antiseptic pro-lifers to do something, actually to act:

In the name of God, do something. Go to the phone and call your congressman. Walk a picket line. Commit civil disobedience. Wear a button. Start or join an action group. This is politics and pressure is what counts now. Pressure the members of Congress. May they not rest in peace!

8

Community and the Church: Commandments for the Long Haul

The discipline of community frees us to go wherever the spirit guides us, even to places we would rather not go. This is the real Pentecost experience.

Henri Nouwen

Community—Our Greatest Need

I grew up in a church that was concerned with apologetics. We were forever worried about making ourselves credible. A lot of effort went into showing that the faith made sense, that being a Christian fulfilled rather than denigrated humanity. We devised all kinds of arguments intended to impress or discredit non-believers: proofs for the existence of God, arguments demonstrating why the human person needs God, and schemata that tried to demonstrate the validity of the church as an institution.

As a young man studying theology I often met this kind of question in a classroom: "Imagine you are traveling on a bus and you meet an atheist. How would you talk about God to such a person?"

Or for those of us who were Roman Catholics, "Imagine you are on a train and meet a Protestant. How would you attempt to show that the Roman Catholic church is the right one?"

Most of these arguments did not get beyond the safety of the classroom. I have been in ministry for fifteen years and have rarely, on bus, train, boat, or plane, met that questioning atheist or Protestant. Most talk on buses and trains revolves around sports, entertainment, politics, and food.

Despite this, the old apologetics had some value; it helped make the faith more credible to those within it.

We still need an apologetics. Its audience, however, has radically changed. If I wrote or taught on apologetics today I would pose the question this way: "Imagine you are sitting at your family table, where some of your own family no longer attend church or take seriously the church's moral teachings. How would you try to prove that faith and Christianity are credible?" We have come a long way from the theoretical atheist on the bus!

The problem of faith in our time is the problem of unbelief among believers. For too many of us faith in Christ is little more than a hangover, toxic residue from a former activity.

What do I perceive as the issue behind this?

The problem, I submit, both within and without, is a problem of credibility; the faith is no longer believable or livable for many in our age. Why? Why is Christ known, but not really believed in?

When I scan religious literature I see various proposed explanations. Conservatives blame our present malaise on lack of prayer and the failure of our age to keep the commandments, pure and simple. If we do not pray and our moral lives are shabby, how can we expect to have a vital faith?

Liberals point to slow renewal within the church as the cause. We are not really renewed, they argue. We still pray to God, talk about God, and worship God in mythical and medieval images. We are schizophrenic in regard to religion. We live modern lives but try to live an old-time religion. Ultimately this freezes God out of all the important areas of life. Religion becomes the great art form and the church becomes the great museum.

Social justice advocates submit that the problem is one of affluence. If Christ made a preferential option for the poor and Christianity is seeing life from the bottom, it is, quite simply, impossible to live as affluently and selfishly as we do and still have a vital connection to Christ.

There is some truth in each of these, but in the end the real reason for the erosion of faith and hope in Christ is something beyond them all. What, singularly, are we missing today within Christianity that could make us credible to the world and to our own families? Community. The greatest need in our time is, as Jim Wallis puts it:

...not simply for *kerygma*, the preaching of the Gospel; nor
for *diakonia*, service on behalf of justice; nor for *charisma*,
the experience of the spirit's gifts; nor even for *propheteia*,
the challenging of the King. The greatest need of our time
is for *koinonia*, the call simply to be church...to offer to the
world a living, breathing, loving community of church.
This is the foundation of all answers. (*The Call to Conversion*, 1982)

In the end, people are as agnostic about faith, Christ, and
the church as they are about the experience of community.
When there is a strong experience of community there is generally a strong faith. For example, wherever today we see a
strong faith we see, invariably, strong community—RCIA
groups, cursillo groups, marriage encounter groups, social justice groups, charismatic groups, Bible study groups, third order groups. These are pockets of fervor within the church and
it is no accident that all of them are linked to strong community experiences.

As well, even in those Christians who are deeply committed
and beyond first fervor, we see that ultimately their strength
issues from community, the Eucharist, common prayer, and a
shared morality and life within the Holy Spirit.

Christianity, in the end, is a communal endeavor. We believe in it when community works, we stop believing in it
when community and family break down. Our primary task
today is to live community. If we can do that, then the visible
body of Christ, the church, will have an incredible resurrection.

Can You Ever Really Leave Home?

Several years ago Carlo Carretto, one of the great spiritual writers of our time, returned to Italy from the Sahara desert after many years as a monk among the Bedouin. He then wrote a spiritual testimony, *I Sought and I Found* (Darton, Longman & Todd, 1984), within which he chronicles his journey toward, and struggles with, God.

He ends the book with a letter, a love letter, addressed to the church, the visible, institutional church. A paraphrase of the opening lines reads like this:

> How much I must criticize you, my church, and yet how much I love you! You have made me suffer more than anyone and yet I owe you more than I owe anyone. I should like to see you destroyed and yet I need your presence. You have given me much scandal and yet you alone have made me understand holiness. Never in the world have I seen anything more obscurantist, more compromised, more false, yet never have I touched anything more pure, more generous, or more beautiful.
>
> Countless times I have felt like slamming the door of my soul in your face—and yet, every night, I have prayed that I might die in your sure arms!
>
> No, I cannot be free of you, for I am one with you, even if not completely you.
>
> Then too, where should I go?
>
> To build another church?
>
> But I cannot build another church without the same defects, for they are my own defects. And again, if I were to build another church, it would be my church, not Christ's church.
>
> No. I am old enough. I know better!

What a magnificent description of the church: flawed, yet divine, mediating God's presence even as it obstructs it!

I have found myself drawing upon this description more and more as I deal with complaints about the institutional church.

What is to be said in the face of the fact that the institutional church is flawed, compromised, corrupted by power, fraught with human weakness and pettiness? What is to be said in the face of the fact that the church has never lived radically and fully the Gospel it preaches?

What is to be said in the face of the fact that, in its darker moments, the church has hurt, and continues to hurt, countless persons? How can it claim credibility and how can it claim to mediate God's presence in the light of this?

These are frequently voiced complaints and often one hears the added comment: "I can deal with God; I can't deal with the church!"

Such complaints are often sincere, though they can also be a rationalization. In either case, however, the facts they point to are true. We cannot deny history and reality. The church has always had, and still has, a dark side. It does not mediate God's presence purely. That is simply a fact.

However, having admitted that, something else must be added. The church, just as humanity itself, is not something abstract. It exists only in real people. We meet the church only in a very particular, historical, concrete enfleshment, that is, in real people with real names, real problems, and real blemishes. What we meet is never the church, but only this or that particular church.

The church is a family, a very concrete and historical one.

This can be, I feel, a helpful perspective to keep in mind. When we are born into a family we bear its birthmark. We can dislike it, we can get angry with it, we can stay away from family celebrations for long periods, we can rage against its faults, and we can be filled with bitterness and protest that it should be more loving, more understanding, less quick to judge and assign guilt—but in the end it is our family and we want to die reconciled with it. Ultimately one of life's non-negotiable imperatives is that one tries to come to peace with one's family. Nobody ever really leaves one's family, even if they die outside of it.

It is the same with the institutional church. It is not God. The institutional church is no more identifiable with God than my historical father is identifiable with God the Father. But, like our historical parents, it is real; it is what we actually meet on earth.

As with our real family, we can dislike it, rage at its faults, and be bitter about its imperfections. We can wish for another family. We can fight with it and stay away for long periods (and sometimes this can be healthy), but in the end we bear its mark on our skin. It is ours; it is the actual and only place in history where we contact the historical Christ.

Because of this, its inexorable reality, we have such strong feelings about it. Like Carretto, there are the times when we feel like slamming the door of our soul in its face, and yet, daily, we pray somehow to die in its arms.

Because of this, like Carretto, we too ultimately realize that we can never really leave the church.

Some of Life's Questions

Rarely do faith, hope, and love come to us pure. Instead, like life itself, they come with mess and doubt, raising huge questions.

Living a human life is not a simple business, especially if one attempts to do this beyond simple instinct. To try to believe in something beyond sight and understanding, to try to place one's trust in something beyond what one can secure, and to try to love non-manipulatively not infrequently raises more questions than answers.

Not to be haunted by doubt, ambiguity, and temptation is to close oneself off from deep thought and feeling. To think and to feel is to be open to many things, darkness as well as light, hatred as well as love, despair as much as hope.

Maurice Merleau-Ponty, the great philosopher of phenomenology, based an entire philosophy on the dictum: Ambiguity is the fundamental fact within experience. That is the philosopher's way of saying that it is not simple out there, that our heads and hearts are full of too many things, and that life is mostly about sorting things out.

And sorting things out is seldom easy. Many voices inside and around us beckon with their own truth: instinctual truth, higher truth, head truth, heart truth, Christian truth, yuppie truth, economic truth, spiritual truth. What is truth?

Which voice speaks truth when so many voices vie with each other? We are called in every direction.

Deep inside us the call is to be a saint, to believe that meaning and happiness lie in generosity and self-forgetfulness; yet other voices, also deep inside us, demand other things; they would have us experience every sensation of the sinner, securing things for ourselves, building a name and a nest.

Which of these voices speaks truth? Does the truth lie in gratitude? Bitterness? Trust? Paranoia? The voices contradict each other and yet each holds its own promise of life, rest, realism, meaning. Small wonder that living can become a tiring enterprise!

So life has its questions. As we struggle to love each other, what is real?

Is the distance between us expanding or is it shrinking?

Are we touching each other's neuroses, or depth?

Are we falling ever more into despair, or is it love?

Do we say the same words too often, or not often enough?

Are we bonded to each other by neurotic pain-giving, or by painful life-giving?

In our obsessions are we bewailing a universal inconsummation, or are we filling in what is lacking in the suffering of Christ?

In our often frayed emotions are we tasting hell, or are we experiencing birth pangs?

Do our frustrations in love unleash our deepest angers, or do they cauterize our worst sins?

Does love itself demand more distance from each other or does it need more mouth-to-mouth resuscitation?

Does passion turn love into idolatry, or into a holy icon?

Is the pain of unrequited love the pain of hell, or is it the pain of purgatory, which feels like hell when heaven cannot be touched?

Questions, love's questions, questions that pose other questions of faith and hope:

Can Christ be believed? Does dying produce new life? Does purgatory turn into heaven? Can what does not seem to be real be, in the end, the most real? Can spirit really triumph over instinct, heart over groin? Can hope find the infinitely small gap through which the future can break into our lives in a new and marvelous way? Can tombs be opened—and reopened—and reopened? Do we really have seventy times seven chances? Will the smell of fresh fish invariably greet us after a night of emptiness? Can our wounds really turn into sure proofs of the resurrection, silencing our doubts as they silenced Thomas? When all the emotions, angers, obsessions, jealousies, insecurities, and immaturities die down, can love really last? Can the ideal really take on flesh?

In the end, that is really the only question. How we answer it will fundamentally fashion or distort us as human beings.

Guidelines for the Long Haul

Several years ago Daniel Berrigan wrote *Ten Commandments for the Long Haul*. It offers advice on how to sustain ourselves until Christ returns.

Here, with the help of various authors, I, too, offer a few commandments designed to help us during the long haul:

Be grateful: never look a gift universe in the mouth!
To be a saint is nothing less than to be warmed and vitalized by gratitude. We owe it to our Creator to appreciate things, to be as happy as we can. Pay for a lovely moment by enjoying it. Resist pessimism and false guilt.

Add this section to the Lord's Prayer: "Give us today our daily bread, and help us to enjoy it without guilt." Keep God central in all.

Don't be naive about God: God will settle for not less than everything!
Distrust all talk about the consolation of religion. Religion puts a belt around you and takes you to where you would rather not be. Get used to virtue; it gives you a constant reminder of what you have missed out on.

Know that God will settle for not less than everything. Demands from God always seem unreasonable. Learn to wrestle with God; you can win, by losing.

Walk forward when possible; when impossible, try to get one foot in front of the next!
Expect long periods of darkness and confusion. Take time to wonder. Take consolation from the fact that Jesus cried, saints sinned, Peter betrayed. See what you see; it is enough to walk

by. Be stubborn as a mule; the only thing that shatters dreams is compromise.

Let ordinary life be enough. Start over often.

Pray that God will hang on to you!
Distrust Gallup polls. Trust prayer. Prayer is an enlargement. Be willing to die a little to be with God. He is dying to be with us. Let your heart, as Henri Nouwen puts it, become the place where the tears of God and the tears of God's children merge and become the tears of hope.

Love: if a life is large enough for love, it is large enough!
Create a space for love in your life. Accept that nothing can be loved too much, though all things can be loved in the wrong way. Make love your eye. Say to those you love: "You, at least, shall not die!"

Know that there are only two potential tragedies to life: not to love and not to tell those whom we love that we love them.

Accept what you are: fear not you are inadequate!
Be just sufficiently fallible to be human. If you are weak, alone, without confidence and without answers, say so; then listen. Accept the torture of a life that is inadequate. Understand your own brand of martyrdom. If you die for a good reason, it is something you can live with!

Don't mummify: let go, so as not to be pushed!
Accept daily deaths. Do not hold on to life as possession. Possessiveness kills enjoyment. Let go of life gracefully. The greatest strength of life is the power to resign it. Death...corruption...resurrection, that is the true rhythm. Keep in mind that it is difficult to distinguish a moment of dying from a moment of birth.

Refuse to take things seriously: call yourself a fool regularly!
Laugh and play and give yourself over to silliness; these are (as C.S. Lewis pointed out) a disgusting and direct insult to the realism, dignity, and austerity of hell. Do not confuse sneering with laughter. Keep in mind that it is easy to be heavy; hard to be light.

Stay with the folks: you are on a group outing!
Do not journey alone. Be "born again" more fully into community. Accept that there are strings attached. To go anywhere in life we have to take along the family, the church, the country, and the human race. Do not be seduced by the false lure of absolute freedom. Learn obedience to community; it humbles, deflates the ego, puts you into purgatory and then into heaven.

Don't be afraid to go soft: redemption lies in tears!
Resist the macho impulse; the person who will not have a softening of the heart will eventually have a softening of the brain. As G.K. Chesterton put it: "The swiftest things are the softest things. A bird is active because a bird is soft. A stone is helpless because a stone is hard. The stone by its nature goes downward, because hardness is weakness. A bird can, of its nature, go upwards; fragility is force."

Know that there are two kinds of darkness one can enter: the fearful darkness of paranoia, which brings sadness, and the fetal darkness of conversion, which brings life.